For God So Loved the World

The Biblical Doctrine of Grace

LARRY HART

For God So Loved the World: The Biblical Doctrine of Grace
Copyright © 2015 by Larry Hart

All Scripture quotations, unless otherwise indicated, are taken from the Holy Bible, *New Revised Standard Version Bible*, NRSV, copyright © 1989 the Division of Christian Education of the National Council of the Churches of Christ in the United States of America. Used by permission. All rights reserved.

Copyrights of Other Bible Versions Used

ESV: *The Holy Bible: English Standard Version*, copyright © 2001 by Good News Publishers. Used by permission. All rights reserved.

NLT: *Holy Bible. New Living Translation,* copyright © 1996, 2004, 2007 by Tyndale House Foundation. Used by permission of Tyndale House Publishers Inc., Carol Stream, Illinois 60188. All rights reserved.

HCSB: *Holman Christian Standard Bible®*, Copyright © 1999, 2000, 2002, 2003, 2009 by Holman Bible Publishers. Used by permission. All rights reserved.

NIV: *New International Version®*, NIV®. Copyright © 1973, 1978, 1984, 2011 by Biblica, Inc.™ Used by permission of Zondervan. All rights reserved worldwide.

RSV: *The Holy Bible: Revised Standard Version*, second edition, copyright © 1946, 1951, 1972 by the Division of Christian Education of the National Council of Churches of Christ in the United States of America. Used by permission. All rights reserved.

NASB: *The New American Standard Bible*, copyright © 1960, 1962, 1968, 1971, 1972, 1973, 1975, 1977, 1995 by The Lockman Foundation. Used by permission. All rights reserved.

CEV: *The Contemporary English Version*, copyright © 1995 by the American Bible Society. Used by permission. All rights reserved.

NJB: *New Jerusalem Bible*, copyright © 1985 by Darton, Longman & Todd Ltd. And Doubleday, a division of Bantam Doubleday Dell Publishing. Used by permission. All rights reserved.

GNT: *Good News Translation*, copyright © 1992 by American Bible Society. Used by permission. All rights reserved.

NKJV: *New King James Version,* copyright © 1979, 1980, 1982 by Thomas Nelson Inc. Used by permission. All rights reserved.

The Message: *The Message: The New Testament in Contemporary English,* copyright © 1993 by Eugene Peterson. Used by permission. All rights reserved.

Cover design and interior design: Kevin Hart

truthaflamepress.com

Table of Contents

Preface 7

Chapter One: Amazing Grace 9

Chapter Two: Grace Is All 13

Chapter Three: Grace in History 27

Chapter Four: Grace in Scripture 43

Chapter Five: Common Grace 73

Chapter Six: Special Grace 105

Chapter Seven: Grace and God's People 127

Chapter Eight: Grace and Southern Baptists 137

Postface 147

Preface

THIS IS A SCANDALOUS BOOK because of its subject-matter. Grace is dangerous. It got Jesus lynched. History's pages are strewn with martyrs over this issue. Saints, all of whom claim to be saved by grace, are still divided as to its precise nature. The actual living of grace is a precious commodity. We may never fully fathom it. Living it seems almost impossible at times, given our common orneriness. But grace—amazing grace—will surely always be the prevailing leitmotif of the Christian symphony. It deserves to be studied, preached, taught, and pursued no matter how imperfectly we may do so.

Grace is the very essence of the Christian message. Ironically, it has also been hotly *debated*, more than perhaps any other doctrine, among Christians themselves. The explanation for this is found in the doctrine of original sin: Our fallenness demonstrates both the need for grace and our inability to fathom it. We too often fail to *show* grace to one another as we debate its nature. We differ, for example, on whether God's saving grace is offered to all people or only to a select group. We argue over whether divine grace can be resisted by fallen humanity. We disagree as to whether someone can depart from saving grace after having experienced it. We even disagree as to the nature of the assurance we can enjoy in our experience of saving grace. We differ widely on prayer and providence, both of which are integral to the biblical doctrine of grace. And, tragically, our internecine battles often obscure our message of grace to an unbelieving world.

This volume is another humble attempt to sound the depths of grace in service of the church's gospel ministry. It is intended for both the classroom and the living room. Pastors, professors, and those they serve can all hopefully benefit from such an exploration. The reflections which follow are not an attempt to exhaust the inexhaustible. We want simply to look across the towering peaks of divine grace and glimpse afresh their grandeur. We will note that the massive ecclesial traditions which have developed down the centuries often differ among themselves and accent diverse aspects of this majestic doctrine. It is not expected that those differences can be dissolved in one modest survey. Nevertheless, now more than ever, the need for greater appreciation and communication is obvious—if for no other reason than to get our message straight in an increasingly diversified world.

Just about every area of vital Christian preaching, teaching, and living will in some way be touched on in this book—that is how all-pervasive the biblical doctrine of grace really is! Hopefully all can glean many useful new perspectives and discover much common ground in such a study. May the God of all grace grant us further theological insight and spiritual transformation in our common quest. Grace to all!

Chapter One:
Amazing Grace

IT WAS MY FIRST PASTORATE. I was a twenty-three-year-old pastor of a small Southern Baptist church of about fifty people in rural southern Indiana, beginning what would become a seven-and-one-half-year seminary pilgrimage, completing my M.Div. and Ph.D. degrees. We had a dynamic radio program every Saturday morning on WPDF, "the voice of the Lincoln hills in Corydon, Indiana—your community station." I would end each program by saying, "That's the Memorial Baptist Church, four miles east of Laconia on the blacktop." The road to our tiny, steepled sanctuary, perched on a hill beside a requisite cemetery, had no name!

Every Saturday morning I would race down those Indiana back roads to arrive in Corydon on time for my weekly live broadcast. Our program came on after "the hospital report," which would announce to the community, for example, that Mabel Jones had had her baby boy last night, and "the swap shop," in which you could advertise anything you wanted to "buy, sell, swap, or trade." (I could never fathom the difference between a swap and a trade.) One man advertised for a wife—and got one! I did my best each week to communicate to all the farmers driving into town and listening to our captivating broadcast the "marvelous grace of our loving Lord."[1] I never dreamed that one day in the jail of that small town, the old state capital, I would have the privilege of seeing that powerful, transforming grace in action in a young man's life.

The caller said, "Brother Larry, would you go visit Bill Schoen over at the jail in Corydon?" I had never met Bill Schoen. But I knew him by reputation and wasn't sure I really wanted to meet him. Bill had a

---
[1] Opening words of the majestic hymn, "Grace Greater than Our Sin." Words, Julia H. Johnston, 1910; Tune, MOODY, Daniel B. Towner, 1910. *Baptist Hymnal*, 1975 ed., (Nashville: Convention Press), hymn no. 164.

major problem with alcohol. Once in a drunken rage he had pushed his paraplegic father in his wheelchair out on a dark country road and left him there to be run over by some unsuspecting driver. When Bill was drunk, he was dangerously mean as well.

Bill had been dating a young girl who attended our church. Her father was an atheist and did not attend our worship services with his wife and daughter. He was also a very large, strong man, who took good care of his family. When he learned that his daughter was dating Bill, he forbad her to see him again. In a drunken rage, Bill put his gun on the rack in his pickup and began driving around the community threatening people as he looked for his girlfriend. He drove out to the farm house and confronted her father. Fisticuffs ensued, and Bill found himself on the ground, bleeding profusely from a badly cut eyelid. The sheriff was called, and Bill found himself in the one-cell jail which housed all the prisoners in Corydon.

Pastors are people too. They often have the same misgivings as their parishioners when confronted by dire situations like this. What do you say to such a young man? Can God really get through to someone like him? I tucked a Four Spiritual Laws booklet in my coat pocket and drove over to the jail, accompanied by one of my faithful deacons (for protection). We stopped in front of the jail and bowed our heads to pray: You pray differently in such situations—with a fervency more akin to the prayers in the Book of Acts!

As we walked down the corridor to the cell, something supernatural happened to me. The Spirit of God fell on me, emptying me of doubt and filling me with compassion for a young man I had never laid eyes on. As we approached the bars of the cell, I noted five or six prisoners milling around in the cell. Bill was easy to spot with his swollen eye and stitches.

I surprised myself with the bold words with which I began our conversation. "Bill Schoen," I said, "I'm Larry Hart, a minister of the gospel of Jesus Christ. Bill, there's no one in the world who can help right now except Jesus Christ." Bill's rapid and cynical response was, "Yeah, but I don't know how to get in touch with him." Reaching into my coat pocket, I replied, "I think I can help you get in touch with him." I began to read Bill the good news of God's saving grace right out of the much used Four Laws booklet. When I came to the question, "Is there any reason why you wouldn't want to receive Christ right now?" Bill's response was simply, "No." I almost replied, "There isn't?" Too often at this juncture people throw out smoke screens like, What about the problem of evil, the hypocrites in the church, the apparent contradictions in the Bible, those who have never heard the gospel, and so forth? But Bill simply said no and bowed his head to pray a prayer of repentance and commitment of his life to Christ. You could hear a pin drop in that jail as we talked and prayed together. It was a powerful moment.

I had just recently attended a Billy Graham School of Evangelism in Chicago. So I was ready for follow-up! We were going over verses of assurance and making plans for follow-up Bible studies when something happened right out of a Hollywood movie script. I looked back and saw someone rolling Bill's father down the corridor toward the cell. The father reached up to his son, saying, "Son, I don't know what I've done wrong." And the son reached down through the bars, saying, "It's alright, Dad, Jesus is going to take care of everything."

Bill faithfully followed through on his Bible studies, transferring his responses to the four Graham follow-up booklets to prison stationery. I would read them and respond back. I moved to another ministry position in Louisville and lost contact with Bill for a few years. But one day at a burger place I saw the young lady who had attended our church, now Bill's wife. I went up to her and asked how she and Bill were doing. She

> Grace is the white-hot, dangerous, holy love of a Sovereign God who loves us enough not only to forgive us but to change us.

said that they were happily married and very much involved in a local Baptist church.

Only the grace of God can bring that kind of transformation. God's grace is not some sentimental idea about a benevolent heavenly "Santa Claus," who winks at our sins. This is the white-hot, *dangerous*, holy love of a Sovereign God who loves us enough not only to forgive us but to change us. Grace is *powerful*. It is undeserved. It is free to us, but infinitely costly to God. It is love all-consuming. And that is what Bill Schoen experienced that day in the Corydon jail.

This is the grace that even the greatest theological minds cannot fully fathom. It is the most important truth any Christian can ever ponder. It is worthy of our best efforts to comprehend, but something we will never fully understand, even through all eternity. Among the teachings of Scripture, it is surely the most edifying to study. We are in for a great adventure!

Chapter Two:
Grace Is All

*Love that goes upward
is worship;
love that goes outward
is affection;
love that stoops
is grace.*
—Donald Grey Barnhouse

*I don't care about my own life.
The most important thing is that I
complete my mission,
the work that the Lord Jesus gave me—
to tell people the Good News
about God's grace.*
—The Apostle Paul, Acts 20:24 NCV

*Amazing grace!
How sweet the sound,
That saved a wretch
Like me!
I once was lost,
But now am found,
Was blind,
But now I see.*
—John Newton

JOHN, THE APOSTLE, may have penned the three most important words ever uttered concerning God: "God is love" (1 John 4:8, 16). This simple three-word sentence is surely "the most daring statement that has ever been made in human language," "the quintessence, the central word of the whole Bible."[1] Linked with the holiness of God as two sides of the same coin, divine love is the theme of biblical redemptive history. It is the old, old story of God's stooping to save the undeserving. It is the story of Jesus and his love. It is the story of amazing grace.

This grace constitutes the uniqueness of the Christian faith, is the essence of the gospel, and is the transforming and liberating power of Christian experience and mission. It is central to our understanding of who God is, what he is like, how he is active among us, and how we should relate to one another.

C. S. Lewis once wandered in late to a conference of comparative religion specialists debating the uniqueness of Christianity among the world's religions. What really sets Christianity apart? After learning the issue in question, he immediately responded, "Oh, that's easy. It's grace."[2] It was this mysterious and powerful divine grace which had ushered the previously atheistic Lewis into the kingdom and transformed him into one of the greatest apologists of the faith. Only of the God of Abraham, Isaac, and Jacob, the God and Father of our Lord Jesus Christ, can it be said that he is pure grace. All other so-called gods pale in comparison with the true and living God of all grace and mercy.

> Grace is God's love in action. The cross is the preeminent sign of God's loving grace.

The greatest revelation of God's love, John explains, is his sending "his only Son into the world that we might live through him," sending him as "the atoning sacrifice for our sins" (1 John 4:9, 10). It is in the concrete terms of incarnation, atonement, and resurrection that the Scriptures present divine grace. Grace is

---

[1] Emil Brunner, *The Christian Doctrine of God*, trans. Olive Wyon (Philadelphia: Westminster, 1950), 183, 199; cited in Jack Cottrell, *What the Bible Says About God the Redeemer* (Joplin, Mo.: College Press, 1987), 323–24.
[2] Cited in: Scott Hoezee, *The Riddle of Grace* (Grand Rapids, Mich.: Eerdmans, 1996), 41–42 and Philip Yancey, *What's So Amazing About Grace?* (Grand Rapids, Mich.: Zondervan, 1997), 45.

God's love in action. The cross is the preeminent sign of God's loving grace. God "proves his love for us in that while we still were sinners Christ died for us" (Rom. 5:8). All roads to a true understanding of the God of all grace ultimately lead to the cross. "Christian faith stands and falls with the knowledge of the crucified Christ, that is, with the knowledge of God *in* the crucified Christ."[3] The cross is literally the crux of Christianity, of the Christian gospel of grace. From this center radiate all the saving effects of God—effects which are ultimately cosmic in scope.

The Source of All Blessing

Behind all saving goodness in life is divine grace. It is "the seed-bed of the entire drama of human salvation" and "the source of all material and spiritual blessings."[4] Grace is the power of God delivering humankind from both spiritual and physical death. Grace forgives, reconciles, loves the unlovely, and changes us into gracious persons, eager to share this supernatural love with others.[5] It is "God's way of empowering the bound will and healing the suffering spirit."[6] Thomas C. Oden summarizes this comprehensive understanding well:

> Grace is an overarching term for all God's gifts to humanity, all the blessings of salvation, all events through which are manifested God's own self-giving. Grace is a divine attribute revealing the heart of the one God, the premise of all spiritual blessing.
>
> Grace is the favor shown by God to sinners. It is the divine goodwill offered to those who neither inherently deserve nor can ever hope to earn it. It is the divine disposition to work in our hearts, wills, and actions, so as actively to communicate God's self-giving love for humanity.[7]

---

[3] Jürgen Moltmann, *The Crucified God*, trans. R. A. Wilson and John Bowden (London: SCM Press, 1974), 65 (Moltmann's italics).
[4] Bruce Demarest, *The Cross and Salvation* (Wheaton, Ill.: Crossway Books, 1997), 49.
[5] Hoezee, *The Riddle of Grace*, 4.
[6] Thomas C. Oden, *The Transforming Power of Grace* (Nashville: Abingdon Press, 1993), 15.
[7] Oden, *The Transforming Power of Grace*, 33, 206.

Grace "contains the essence of the gospel as a drop of water can contain the image of the sun."[8]

In biblical parlance grace encompasses both divine and human generosity. Grace summarizes all sacrificial giving that enriches life and furthers God's kingdom. And grace becomes thereby a referent to (1) the act of giving, (2) the gift itself, (3) the attitude of the giver, and (4) the blessing of the receiver. In fact, the term blessing itself is a fitting rendering of grace in most biblical contexts. Even our response of gratitude itself is a form of grace. Thus, grace is a circle moving from heaven to earth and back again! We are blessed by God, and we, therefore, bless him:

> Bless the Lord, O my soul,
>   and all that is within me,
>   bless his holy name (Ps. 103:1).

> Blessed be the God and Father of our Lord Jesus Christ, who has blessed us in Christ with every spiritual blessing in the heavenly places (Eph. 1:3).

> We want you to know, brothers and sisters, about the grace of God that has been granted to the churches of Macedonia ... a wealth of generosity on their part ... begging us earnestly for the privilege of sharing [lit. the grace (*charin*) and the fellowship (*koinōnian*)] in this ministry to the saints (2 Cor. 8:1–4).

In fact, Paul referred to his collection for the beleaguered saints of Jerusalem as "this generous undertaking [lit. grace]" (2 Cor. 8:6, 7), and promised the Corinthians: "And God is able to make all grace ['every blessing' NRSV] abound to you, so that in all things at all times, having all that you need, you will abound in every good work" (2 Cor. 9:8 NIV[1984]).

There is "abundant joy" (2 Cor. 8:2) in this kind of "cheerful" giving (2 Cor. 9:7). "God loves a cheerful giver" and will enrich them in every way, so that their generosity will produce much gratitude (*eucharistia*; note the term *grace*, *charis*, in this word) to God (vv. 7, 11, 12). Jesus

---

[8] Philip Yancey, *What's So Amazing About Grace?*, 13.

himself taught that our giving can never outstrip God's giving back to us (Luke 6:38). This is the "seed-faith" lifestyle which Oral Roberts recommended to the church for decades! Thus, grace literally is the source of all blessing. There is also a freedom that comes with the graced life.

Grace and Freedom

Paul, *the* theologian of grace in the eyes of many, discovered that grace brings a freedom to one's life which the law could never provide. "For freedom Christ has set us free," he exhorted the feckless and faithless Galatians who wanted "to be justified by the law" (Gal. 5:1, 4). Paul had been down that road. He warned: "[You] have cut yourselves off from Christ; you have fallen from grace" (v. 4). He knew that it is only "through the Spirit" and "by faith" that we achieve true righteousness (v. 5).

Originally, F. F. Bruce wanted to title his overview of Paul, "Paul: Apostle of the Free Spirit."[9] How aptly descriptive of Paul! He was considered dangerous—many times by his own compatriots in the gospel (Gal. 2)! Some "false believers" were even sent to "spy on the freedom we have in Christ Jesus" (v. 4), he said. There will always be those religionists in the church that Chuck Swindoll calls, in effect, "grace killers."

> They kill freedom, spontaneity, and creativity; they kill joy as well as productivity. They kill with their words and their pens and their looks. They kill with their attitudes far more often than with their behavior. There is hardly a church or Christian organization or Christian school or missionary group or media ministry where such danger does not lurk. The amazing thing is that they get away with it, day in and day out, without being confronted or exposed.[10]

These folk are manipulative, intolerant, judgmental, narrow-minded, and bullying. "The bondage that results would be criminal were it not so subtle and wrapped in such spiritual-sounding garb."[11] Preach or live grace for very long around such people and you are sure to encounter

---

[9] F. F. Bruce, *Paul: Apostle of the Heart Set Free* (Grand Rapids, Mich.: Eerdmans, 1977).
[10] Charles R. Swindoll, *The Grace Awakening* (Dallas: Word, 1990), 3.
[11] Swindoll, *The Grace Awakening*, 3–4.

their wrath. Such folk lynched Jesus. And they harassed Paul wherever he traveled. He had learned to "travel light" in at least two senses.

Eugene Peterson's insightful commentary on Galatians effectively explicates Paul's freedom in grace.[12] Peterson initially embarked on his journey through Galatians because he found the very people he lived with as pastor to be disturbingly unfree.[13] He characterizes his whole ministry in grace-terms: "My job is not to solve people's problems or make them happy, but to help them see the grace operating in their lives."[14]

Paul evinced tremendous confidence in the Holy Spirit of grace. He knew that without the gracious activity of the Spirit in our lives we are nobodies heading nowhere. But led by the Spirit, we are world change-agents, being continually transformed ourselves! His whole ethic was, in effect, "What does the Holy Spirit think about this? What is his leading here?"[15] It is no accident that Paul's freedom epistle (Galatians) is replete with references to the Spirit and to grace.

> The evangelical impulse has always been to turn to Paul to explicate the doctrine of grace.

Further, only grace could explain how Paul, "the prisoner of Christ Jesus" (Eph. 3:1 NASB), could be free even in the Roman prison from which he wrote of his apostolic commission as being a result of God's grace (Eph. 3:1–13, esp. vv. 2, 7, and 8). I can add my own personal testimony to that of Paul and all ministers of the gospel since his day, that I am a servant of the Word only by "the gift of God's grace that was given me by the working of his power" (Eph. 3:6–7). But nowhere does the apostle give fuller expression to the doctrine of God's variegated grace (see 1 Peter 4:10) than in his majestic Roman epistle.

---

[12] Eugene H. Peterson, *Traveling Light* (Colorado Springs: Helmers & Howard, 1988).
[13] Peterson, *Traveling Light*, 11.
[14] Eugene H. Peterson, *The Contemplative Pastor* (Dallas: Word, 1989), 13.
[15] See George T. Montague, *The Holy Spirit: Growth of a Biblical Tradition* (New York: Paulist Press, 1976), 199–200.

Romans as the Template of the Biblical Doctrine of Grace

The evangelical impulse has always been to turn to Paul to explicate the doctrine of grace. It is a legitimate instinct in view of the theological influence of Paul on the theology of the church in general and on our gospel parlance in particular. Although it could be cogently argued that to Jesus alone belongs this distinctive teaching, it is also obviously true that Paul has provided the terminology for the church's perennial theology of grace.

James D. G. Dunn masterfully summarizes Paul's contribution:

> Among the most innovative features which shaped Christian theology for all time are the key terms which Paul introduced. Above all we should think of "gospel," "grace," and "love"—gospel as the good news of Christ focusing in his death and resurrection, grace as epitomizing the character of God's dealings with humankind, love as the motive of divine giving and in turn the motive for human living. Between them, in their specialist Christian usage, these words sum up and define the scope and character of Christianity as no other three words can. And that specialist Christian usage, in each case, we owe entirely to Paul.[16]

A strong case can be made for Dunn's assertion that "Paul was the first and greatest Christian theologian."[17] And Ben Witherington's reservations notwithstanding,[18] surely Dunn is right when he argues that if "we wish to grasp at and dialogue with the mature theology of Paul we cannot do better than take Romans as a kind of template on which to construct our own statement of Paul's theology."[19]

Popular author Phil Yancey has written one of the most engaging and challenging explorations of grace in recent years. Acknowledging the many persons who contributed to his volume, he notes, upon reflection,

---

[16] James D. G. Dunn, *The Theology of Paul the Apostle* (Grand Rapids, Mich.:Eerdmans, 1998), 733.
[17] Dunn, *The Theology of Paul the Apostle*, 2.
[18] Ben Witherington III, *The Paul Quest: The Renewed Search for the Jew of Tarsus* (Downers Grove, Ill.: InterVarsity Press, 1998), 279.
[19] Dunn, *The Theology of Paul the Apostle*, 25–26.

how formative Paul's Roman epistle has been in his own understanding and presentation of grace:

> Come to think of it, I should also thank the apostle Paul who, in his magnificent letter to the Romans, taught me everything I know about grace and gave me the outline to this book as well. I describe "ungrace," attempt to fathom grace, deal with objections that arise during that process, and discuss how grace is lived out in a cold, flinty world—precisely the progression of Romans.[20]

Max Lucado sounds a similar note in his own popular explication of grace: "Romans is the grandest treatise on grace ever written."[21] As with the generations of Augustine, Luther, Wesley, and Barth, so with the contemporary church: Romans continues to demonstrate its spiritual power. If there is one word that summarizes the gospel, it is *grace*. And if there is one epistle that effectively summarizes Paul's understanding of the gospel of grace, it would surely be the Roman epistle, "The Gospel According to Paul." Luther called it "the chief part of the New Testament and the very purest Gospel."[22]

Romans appears to be carefully structured. The introduction (Rom. 1:1–17) broaches virtually every major theme developed in the epistle and provides an apt précis with the words: "I am not ashamed of the gospel, because it is the power of God for the salvation of everyone who believes: first for the Jew, then for the Gentile. For in the gospel a righteousness from God is revealed, a righteousness that is by faith from first to last, just as it is written: 'The righteous will live by faith'" (Rom. 1:16–17 NIV[1984]).

Romans 1:18–3:31 outlines the need for the gospel, for grace, in terms of the culpability of both Jew and Gentile. It is perhaps the most extensive treatment of sin in all the Scriptures. Paul embeds within this section a paragraph-long sentence which is the epistle in nuce (Rom. 3:21–26). It is the quintessence of Paul's understanding of the gospel. Then be-

---

[20] Yancey, *What's So Amazing About Grace?* 7–8.
[21] Max Lucado, *In the Grip of Grace* (Dallas: Word, 1996), xiii.
[22] Martin Luther, *Commentary on the Epistle to the Romans*, trans. J. Theodore Mueller (Grand Rapids, Mich.: Kregel, 1954), xiii.

ginning with chapter four (primarily on Abraham as our example and father in the faith) and on through the unit comprised of chapters five through eight (Paul's essential doctrine of salvation), Paul explicates his gospel of grace culminating with chapters nine through eleven, which deal with the role of Israel in God's plan of redemption. Also, in these three chapters we have some of the most important materials relating to election and predestination—key doctrines still debated in the quest for a greater understanding of divine grace. Finally, the epistle culminates with the closing practical chapters (twelve through sixteen).

In our journey of exploration through the heart of the Christian faith, we will return, as has the church all through her history, to the Roman epistle for our bearings and for further doctrinal data. And just as with Paul in Romans, we must first grasp our need for grace before we can fully appreciate and apprehend it.

The Need for Grace

When Anselm explained to his mythical pupil, Boso, the necessity of the atonement, he made this pointed assertion: "You have not yet considered what a heavy weight sin is" (*Cur Deus Homo*, I, 21). Grace can only be clearly seen in relation to this "heavy weight" called sin.

In their most lucid moments, most people are willing to admit that there is something drastically wrong with humankind. The whole of western society is undergoing a virtual paradigm shift at present, in part, as a response to just this fact. The optimism of the modern era, dating back to the Enlightenment, is fast giving way to the pessimism of the postmodern era. Modern humanity was confident in its intelligence and technology to solve all its problems. Instead, we have created even more perilous problems and are no closer to the truth than when the rationalistic experiment first began with Kant. Now with the emerging postmodern mentality, it is evident that many have given up the idea of absolute truth. They have also despaired of technology's providing the saving answers for which we all quest.[23] What *is* the answer to the global inhumanity of our day?

The fundamental problem of the human race, according to Scripture, is found in one three-letter word: sin. It is the explanation for the most profound social and personal ills we face. And there is only one solution: grace. We can pass laws against drugs, racism, and abuses of all kinds, and build a virtual police state to enforce these laws. But only a fundamental change of the human heart will achieve our common goals.

The overarching story of the Scriptures can be subsumed under the classical Christian rubrics of Creation, Fall, and Redemption. Creation tells us the *great news* of a good God who creates a good universe as well as humankind in his own image (Gen. 1, 2). In this regard, one could say that the "problem of good" is introduced with this particular biblical doctrine. How can there be so much good in us when we are so fatally flawed? *Schindler's List* poignantly illustrates this truth by portraying how the same German authorities that engineered the Holocaust could also be seen as possessing artistic sensitivities and genuine affection and compassion for spouses and children.

The Fall points us to the *bad news* of the introduction of sin into the human race, with all the catastrophic effects that have ensued therefrom (Gen. 3–11). The "problem of evil" comes to the fore as transcendent evil entices humans to personal evil, which results in the curse of the creation itself. It is out of this stygian darkness that the blinding light of redemption emerges.

The Lord God announces the enmity between the serpent and the woman and between his offspring and hers (Gen. 3:15). He also makes garments from the skins of slain animals to cover the shame of the primal couple (Gen. 3:21). Then, with the call of Abram (Gen. 12), the sacred history of redemption begins. It is the *good news* of God's saving *grace*. Charles Colson and Nancy Pearcey have demonstrated that merely explicating this amazing biblical message of creation, fall, and redemption—and

---

[23] See David F. Wells, *No Place for Truth* (Grand Rapids, Mich.: Eerdmans, 1993).

tracing the lines of contemporary application of these truths—is the most powerful apologetic the church has.[24] This Christian worldview carries its own power of recommendation *because it is the truth*. It alone makes sense of our lives. It alone tells the story of amazing grace.

According to the Bible, we are all, without exception, *outlaws*. We have violated every moral and ethical precept which our vertical relationship with God and our horizontal relationships with one another and with the creation itself entail. The Ten Commandments (Ex. 20:1–17) and the Love Command (Matt. 22:34–40; compare Deut. 6:5; Lev. 19:18) are the touchstones which also point us to our need of saving grace. We are lawless (1 John 3:4). We are ungodly (Rom. 1:18–25). We see God as an intruder in our lives. If we acknowledge that he exists at all, it is only for our own glory and pleasure (rather than our existing for his glory and pleasure). We are spiritually ignorant (Rom. 1:18–23) and idolatrous (Rom. 1: 24–25) in our ungodliness. We are also unrighteous, consumed with sins of the human flesh (Rom. 1:26–27) and sins of the human spirit (Rom. 1:28–32). This condition of humankind is universal in scope (Rom. 2:1–3:20).[25]

> According to the Bible, we are all, without exception, outlaws.

And the results of sin have been catastrophic. *Physical death* has a sting which can only be removed by grace (1 Cor. 15:55–57). *Spiritual death*, in terms of alienation, spiritual blindness, and moral servitude, can only be overturned by the reconciling, regenerating power of grace. And *eternal death* can only be personally averted by humbly accepting the gift of saving grace.[26]

---

[24] Charles Colson and Nancy Pearcey, *How Now Shall We Live?* (Wheaton, Ill.: Tyndale, 1999).
[25] See Dale Moody, *The Word of Truth* (Grand Rapids, Mich.: Eerdmans, 1981), 275–7; David L. Smith, *With Willful Intent* (Wheaton, Ill.: Victor Books, 1994), 314–26; Larry D. Hart, *Truth Aflame* (Grand Rapids, Mich.: Zondervan, 2005), 269–72.
[26] See Hart, *Truth Aflame*, 272–76.

The opening verses of Paul's Colossian epistle perhaps best communicate the powerful effects of the church's message of grace in a contemporary culture not unlike that of Paul's own day. The apostle refers to the Colossians' "faith in Christ Jesus," their "love in the Spirit," and their "hope" of heaven—all of which are the result of the supernatural fruit and growth of "the word of truth, the gospel," "the grace of God" (Col. 1:3–8). This triumphant, inexhaustible divine grace is the ocean into which we will dip our toe in the humble explorations that follow. What will become immediately apparent is how all-encompassing the biblical doctrine of grace actually is. We eventually are faced with the most fundamental of life's questions: Who is God? How does he relate to us? How does he save us? How then should we live?

Who Is God?

First and foremost, grace *points us to God*. It prompts us to ask, Who is this God of grace and glory? What is he like? How could he be so gracious? We begin to explore the love, mercy, goodness, and grace of God—divine attributes, the theologians call them. The biblical doctrine of grace continually reminds us of God's priority. Life is ultimately about God, not about us. His grace precedes all that we ever do, say, or think. His preeminence entails his prevenience. We are forced to dive into the ocean of God's essence, names, attributes, and triunity.

How Does God Relate to Us?

How does the God of sovereign grace relate to his creation? Scriptures teach a divine benevolence toward all of creation. Beyond this, they portray a God who preserves, governs, and guides. How might this correlate with our prayers? Again, there is a diversity of perspectives, but most in some way allow for authentic interaction between God and humanity. Thus, the Bible presents both a universal common grace as well as a supernatural saving grace that in part involves answered prayer.

How Does God Save Us?

The ecumenical creeds (e.g., Apostles' and Nicene) have expressed for centuries what the churches hold in common concerning special, saving grace. But beyond this broader perspective lies a surprising diversity of detail. The doctrine of redemption is in purview here—what the churches teach concerning sin, Christ, faith, hope, and love.[27] It is in this arena that the dialogue among believers gets most interesting! However, doctrinal concerns are only half the problem. It is the *living out* of grace that is all too often neglected, to the diminishing of the church's life and witness.

How Then Should We Live?

The biblical doctrine of grace also has to do with *the attitudes and actions of God's people.* Grace has everything to do with how we relate to one another in Christian community and how we relate to the world around us. God bestows "grace gifts" (*charismata*) for the building up of the church. In a bold and merciful love, we are empowered to reach out to the needs of our neighbor and give concrete expression to God's glorious grace. Thus, the doctrines of grace are all-encompassing.

Grace Is All

The study of divine grace (charismology) touches upon the doctrines of God, providence, prayer, Christology, atonement, pneumatology (the Holy Spirit), soteriology (salvation), ecclesiology (the church), and even eschatology (last things). It demonstrates the unity of these doctrines and explores their dynamics. Ultimately, use must be made of all the classical theological disciplines: historical theology, biblical theology, systematic theology, and pastoral theology. The ultimate purpose of such a study must be *the transformation of our lives by God's amazing grace!*

A good way to begin our journey is with a quick glance backward to see how the church has wrestled with these issues throughout her

---

[27] For my own explication of these rubrics see *Truth Aflame*, chs. 6–10.

history. Heretical, schismatic movements forced the church to get her act together in this arena. The early centuries witnessed a number of threats to gospel fidelity, all of which forced the church to refine her conceptions of grace. Centuries later she would become aware of the need for further refinements. And today we still struggle with the challenge "to contend for the faith that was once for all delivered to the saints," since the perennial proclivity is to "pervert the grace of our God" and to "deny our only Master and Lord, Jesus Christ" (Jude 2–4 ESV).

We owe a great debt to the church fathers of the first five centuries. In their battles with Marcionism, Arianism, Donatism, and Pelagianism, they hammered out a biblical orthodoxy we still confess today in the Apostles' and Nicene creeds. Among these fathers St. Augustine would emerge as the theological giant whose powerful influence continues to this day. In large measure, the touchstone was already in place for the churches' use in subsequent centuries. Today, a Post-Reformation world is witnessing a rediscovery of common ground among the disparate Protestant, Catholic, Orthodox, and Pentecostal/charismatic traditions. It is a time of prodigious peril and promise. And the felt need for divine grace is greater than ever.

Chapter Three:
Grace in History

THE CHURCH OWES A GREAT DEBT to the heretics. Quite often they have been the ones who have forced us to do our theological homework, to get our act straight. Sometimes contemporary heretics help remind us that the ones we read about in our history texts were flesh and blood folk as well. More often than not, these misled religionists had a legitimate concern, but simply came up with the wrong answers. In our day, for example, in an attempt to recover and fully appreciate the complete humanity of Jesus in his historical context, some scholars have simply lost sight of his full divinity and allowed his miracles and bodily resurrection to drop out of the biblical portrait. The same is true of the Bible. It is a fully human book, yet supernaturally breathed out by God. In seeking to assert the former, some have too often denied the latter.

> The church owes a great debt to the heretics.

In my own city, dominated by a robust brand of charismatic Christianity, a teaching has emerged which on the surface seems simply to be calling for including all persons as candidates of divine grace. Unfortunately, as often happens in the history of Christian theology, grace has become distorted into a rather grotesque new form of universalism in which it is asserted that virtually everyone, save a few atheists, is already saved! The concern for an inclusive spirit is legitimate; the assertion of universal salvation is heretical.

To begin our historical journey, we will take note of perhaps the four greatest heresies of the patristic period (the church of the first five centuries): Marcionism, Arianism, Donatism, and Pelagianism. It was primarily in response to these aberrations that the fathers of our faith, as already mentioned, hammered out the theology we find distilled in the ecumenical creeds we confess as our common faith today. And the first great heretic of the church was Marcion.

Faith of Our Fathers: The Church of the First Five Centuries

Had Marcion (*ca.* 80–160) stayed with orthodoxy, he could have been the John Wesley of his day. Not content with merely teaching his Gnostic ideas privately among his followers, Marcion, great organizer that he was, established a rival church with its own canon of Scripture. The result was that the fathers were nudged further down the road of developing their own Canon, Creed, Church, and Christology.

Marcion was haunted by the problem of sin and evil. Plagued by a personal struggle with sexual immorality, which resulted in his being excommunicated from the church by his own bishop father, Marcion fell into the trap of the Gnosticism of his day which taught a false dualism between "pure" spirit and "evil" matter. Bodily life in general and sexuality in particular Marcion saw as inherently evil.[1] Further, he had trouble accepting the God of the Hebrew Scriptures. Reacting to the legalism found in many quarters of the Judaism and Christianity of his day, he taught a dualism of love versus justice. Instead of an alienated humanity as a result of the fall (original sin), Marcion taught an *alien god*. God the creator and lawgiver is humanity's nemesis; he was conquered, however, by the God of love revealed in Jesus. This is the true God—the God of love and grace and forgiveness. Harold O. J. Brown summarizes it well:

> The creator of this world is alien to the true God and alien to spiritual man. He is the Yahweh of the Old Testament, a wild god, one who can rage, make mistakes, and repent, one who knows

---

[1] In fairness to Marcion though, Augustine himself seemed to express a rather low view of sexuality, probably due in large measure to his pre-conversion struggle with sexual immorality. More than one patristic father evinced a low, unbiblical view of humanity as male and female.

nothing of grace, but only strict justice. This God is responsible for the misery of man; and he gave us the Old Testament with all its features....[2]

Thus, the "jealous God" (Ex. 20:5) of the Hebrew Bible, who leads his people into battle, ordering them to slaughter entire populations, requiring bloody cultic sacrifices, and demanding strict justice, is our enemy.

Far above this vindictive god, is the "foreign god," the "unknown god." This is the God of the Christian gospel, who forgives even the worst of sinners—the loving, peaceful, infinitely good God of love and grace. Thus, according to Marcion, Jesus was neither the Jews' Messiah nor the Christians' Incarnate Logos. He was not born of the Virgin Mary in Bethlehem. He simply appeared, full grown, in the synagogue of Capernaum, teaching and preaching the gospel of grace as the emissary of the Father.

Having jettisoned the Hebrew Scriptures, Marcion collected his own Scriptures, which consisted of ten of Paul's letters (omitting the Pastorals) and the gospel narrative of Paul's missionary companion, Luke. Marcion carefully edited these works to remove any remnants of Old Testament teachings, and he placed Galatians at the head of his canon. For Marcion, Paul was the only true apostle, who had received his gospel by a special revelation that set him apart from Peter, James, and John, for example. And Galatians, a "wealth of riches" with nothing "to compare with it," was the sine qua non of the Marcionite Bible. Marcion stood in wonder and awe before the Pauline doctrine of grace—salvation by grace alone through faith alone.[3]

The alert reader will already be aware of the fact that the contemporary church is full of quasi-Marcionites. Too many Christians find little, if any, use for the Old Testament, secretly, if not openly, seeing two different gods being taught. Too many of us also have a biblically

---
[2] Harold O. J. Brown, *Heresies* (Garden City, New York: Doubleday, 1984), 61.
[3] See Jaroslav Pelikan, *The Christian Tradition: A History of the Development of Doctrine: 1. The Emergence of the Catholic Tradition* (100–600) (Chicago: The University of Chicago Press, 1971), 112–13.

unworthy view of our bodily lives and our sexuality. Too many of us have never fully embraced Christ's complete *humanity*, which is just as central to our redemption as his divinity. And in charismatic circles, we sometimes find Marcion's false hermeneutic in a teaching which elevates Paul's writings (based on "revelation knowledge") above the rest of the New Testament canon.

But the most important issue Marcion raises for our purposes is that of the centrality of grace. Without doubt, his doctrine of two gods, his rejection of the Old Testament, his dualism, and his docetism (denial of Jesus' full humanity) will not wash with those who hold to any semblance of orthodoxy. But Marcion's quest for grace should resonate with all of us. Justo L. González provides us with this reminder of the lessons we can learn from Marcion:

> His call for a new discovery of the unmerited grace of God was necessary and relevant in the midst of the legalism that threatened to sweep the church. But his denial of God's action in the history of Israel and his dualistic interpretation of the history of salvation made the church attack him with such vigor that the positive values of his doctrines did not receive the attention that they merited.[4]

The battle for grace continues in every generation. Even in Christian circles the good news of God's grace is often eclipsed by shallow legalisms, spiritual pride, denominational and theological exclusiveness, and superficial relationships. All these make it even that much more difficult for the unchurched to receive the gospel we preach. We focus on ourselves rather than on the God of grace and glory who has redeemed us in Christ. The next heresy we must consider, in its own way, raises these same issues. Who's doing the saving? God or us?

> *Marcionism put forth another church with another Bible and another gospel.*

---

[4] Justo L. González, *A History of Christian Thought*, Vol. 1 (Nashville: Abingdon, 1970), 144.

Marcionism put forth another church with another Bible and another gospel. Arianism was perhaps an even greater threat, however, because it almost became the official teaching of the patristic church. Had it not been for the courageous and heroic efforts of that great champion of the faith, Athanasius, Arianism might have won the day. From a careful study of the church's struggle with Arianism we learn how essential the doctrines of the Trinity and the Incarnation are to the biblical doctrine of grace.

Arius (*ca.* 256–336) initially was a presbyter in an urban church in Alexandria. Attempting to guard the complete transcendence of God as the supreme monarch, Arius ended up denying divine omnipresence and incarnation. In defending God's *eminence* (God's being infinitely superior to and "other than" all that he has made), he denied God's *immanence* (God's being everywhere present to all that he has made). Similar to the neo-platonic thought of his day, Arius' concept was that God, the Supreme Being, *created* a "deputy god," as it were, to bring forth the created order (comparable to the Demiurge of Gnosticism). Jesus was that deputy god. "There was a time when he was not," Arius would argue. So God created Jesus and then through Jesus created the universe. Jesus then becomes a *tertium quid*, a "third something," neither completely God nor completely human.

Athanasius (*ca.* 296–373), bishop of Alexandria from 328 to his death in 373, argued that Arianism blinds us to the truth of who God is and how he saves us in Christ Jesus. But his battle for the gospel of grace was not an easy one: He spent seventeen of his forty-five years as bishop in five different exiles. He literally put his life on the line for the faith of the church. According to Athanasius, grace means that God stoops to save us in the Incarnation. The doctrines of the Trinity and the Incarnation are grace doctrines. They are central to the church's message of redemption. And in our own day we have had to take a similar stand against cults like the Jehovah's Witnesses with their Arian Christology and so-called Christian theologians who would reject out of hand

Christ's divinity and God's triune nature. Most recently, we have seen the willingness on the part of some to part with the deity of Christ and doctrine of the Trinity in an effort to build bridges toward Islam. To do so is to give up the gospel of grace.[5] But grace is more than something to believe in and to experience. It is something we are to continually extend to others and share among ourselves as believers. Donatism, our next great heresy, raised this issue.

The Donatists, a group of native African Christians, in what is now Algeria, were a holiness movement, and the besetting sin of all holiness movements, going back to the Pharisees themselves, is to become a graceless, mean-spirited, legalistic sect which excludes others, who are deemed inferior and unacceptable. Onto this scene stepped a theological giant of the church who addressed both this heresy and the Pelagian heresy which follows: St. Augustine (354–430). Augustine of Hippo, bishop of this North African church, refused to accept the schism brought on by the Donatists, who exluded those who in their weakness had denied their faith to avoid the Diocletian persecutions. Further, they denied the validity of all the baptisms administered by those ministers who ultimately folded in the face of persecution.

Augustine, on the other hand, maintained a pastoral touch and defended the doctrines of grace. The church is a mixed body of saints and sinners, he would argue. The wheat and the tares grow together, and the separation of good and evil will only take place at the end of the age (Matt. 13:24–31). Our holiness is derivative, not inherent. Christ himself is our holiness (1 Cor. 1:30). Only by the grace of Christ do we experience our present justification and sanctification and our future perfection. The personal qualities of the minister do not dictate the authenticity of our baptism, as the Donatists argued, but only the grace of Christ himself. "Responding to this approach, Augustine argued that Donatism laid excessive emphasis upon the qualities of the

---

[5] See Timothy George's excellent *Is the Father of Jesus the God of Muhammad?* (Grand Rapids: Zondervan, 2002).

human agent, and gave insufficient weight to the grace of Christ."⁶ In effect, Augustine was exhorting, "Get your eyes off of fallen humanity and onto our gracious God!"

The same kind of ungrace is found in our churches today. We bury our wounded rather than restore them. We too often treat divorced people as second-class citizens. We raise our superior noses at those who differ from us in doctrine and experience. "Change your outward appearance and behavior," we say to the outsider, "and we will accept you." There is a discipline to be maintained, and there are doctrinal parameters outside of which we dare not stray. But the kind, pastoral touch of an Augustine is our model here, not that of the Donatists.

> The battle Augustine waged with Pelagianism is one of the key events in the history of the church's doctrine of grace.

But perhaps the most significant patristic heresy for us to consider, in terms of present day debates concerning the nature of divine grace, is Pelagianism. Here again, Augustine plays a major role—both then and now!

The battle Augustine waged with Pelagianism is one of the key events in the history of the church's doctrine of grace. Pelagius, a British lay theologian who came to Rome around the year 400, taught that humanity has total freedom of will and therefore total responsibility for sin. His concepts of the freedom of the will, the nature of sin, the nature of grace, and the basis of salvation all flew in the face of what the Scriptures teach. Pelagius' concern for the moral laxity of the church was legitimate, but his answer to the problem was fatally defective. As an ascetic, Pelagius taught that Christians should pursue self-improvement according to the Old Testament law and the example of Christ. God

---

⁶ Alister E. McGrath, *Historical Theology* (Malden, Mass.: Blackwell, 1998), 76.

gave laws he expected us to obey, and he asks nothing of us that we cannot achieve. No divine grace is needed because there is no inherent weakness in humanity.

Augustine, on the other hand, taught original sin in terms of our will being biased toward sin. We still have freedom, but that free will has been weakened and incapacitated (though not eliminated or destroyed) by sin. Using a scales analogy, Augustine would say that the scales (our wills) still work even though they are biased toward evil. Pelagius would argue that the scales are perfectly balanced. With this concept, Pelagius takes the next step in calling for a rigid moral authoritarianism which allows only the morally perfected to enter the church. We are born sinless and are under divine obligation to live morally perfect lives.

Augustine's teaching reflected the biblical perspective on sin as a state of being in which all of us are born. Sin (singular) produces sins (individual acts). Pelagius omitted the former. Augustine saw grace as healing the hereditary *disease* of sin, enabling us to recognize God and our need of him and to respond to his gracious offer of redemption. Christ liberates us by his grace from the *power* of sin which holds us captive. And divine grace releases us from the *guilt* of sin, a juridical concept. In contrast, Pelagius taught that we are justified on the basis of our merits. We are saved by imitating Christ's example.

Augustine would go further by saying that the basis of our justification is God's divine promise of grace, but that even that promise itself is left to God's prerogative. Predestination, in Augustine's view, entailed God's eternal decision to save some and not others from the damning and debilitating effects of sin. Many of his contemporaries (and successors) found this double-edged predestination view unacceptable.

Augustine's theological pilgrimage also raises another foundational issue related to the biblical doctrine of grace. The early Augustine thought of the interrelation of God and humanity in terms of a *synergism*, that is, God's and humanity's working together. In this view, we are not totally passive in the redemptive process. However, after years of battling against the Pelagian heresy, Augustine moved to a position of *monergism*, that God is the sole actor in redemption. Some see this as an overreaction to Pelagianism. But more on this later. In any event, the council of Carthage (418) decided in favor of Augustine's views on sin and grace and condemned Pelagianism.[7]

The Middle Ages and the Renaissance (ca. 500–1500)

During the Middle Ages and the Renaissance, the church further developed the theology of Augustine in a more systematic direction. Augustine, the pastor, formulated his ideas in a polemical environment, whereas the theologians of the Middle Ages sought to provide foundations and consolidation, all of which prepared the way for the Reformation debates to follow. Two significant developments were "The Modern Way" (*Via Moderna*) and "The Modern Augustinian School" (*Schola Augustiniana Moderna*). The former leaned more in the Pelagian direction, understanding God's covenant as investing saving value to our efforts at "doing the best that lies within us." These works themselves carried no saving significance. But God's gracious covenant vested them with saving significance. Predictably, the Augustinian response of "The Modern Augustinian School" was that we have absolutely no internal resources to initiate or persist in such a process. Salvation is totally the work of our Sovereign Lord.[8]

Another theological giant emerged in the Middle Ages, who continues to cast a long shadow down to our own day: Thomas Aquinas (*ca.* 1225–74). This brilliant philosopher/theologian put forth one of the most intriguing conceptions of grace in the history of Christian theology. Aquinas differentiated between nature and grace, the natural and the supernatural. In Aquinas' understanding, nature can be known

---
[7] The above analysis of Pelagianism and Augustine is based on the excellent summary and analysis provided by Alister E. McGrath in his *Historical Theology*, 35–37, 79–85 and *Christian Theology*, 2d ed. (Cambridge, Mass.: Blackwell, 1997), 426–32.
[8] Again, see McGrath, *Historical Theology*, 106–08 for a more detailed summary.

by unaided reason alone, since in his view reason is untainted by sin. However, the supernatural can only be known by grace, that is, through divinely given revelation. Thus, Aquinas could use Aristotelian reason to demonstrate the existence of God, but would appeal to God's gracious revelation alone as the basis of our knowledge of the Trinity and the saving significance of Christ, for example. In other words, Aquinas utilized Augustine's theology when it came to grace and the supernatural. In relating nature and grace, Aquinas would argue that grace does not contradict or supersede nature, but perfects it. Some would see a Pelagian danger in this nature/grace differentiation in terms of Aquinas' confidence in an unaided reason unaffected by sin.

Scholastic theology in general made numerous distinctions within grace which have persisted down to the present. Different "kinds" of grace were expounded: (1) justifying grace, which elevates us to the realm of grace and the supernatural; (2) sanctifying grace, which brings holiness and communion with God; (3) gratuitous grace, not bound to any predetermined channel; (4) habitual grace, which is a permanent grace; and (5) actual grace, enabling extraordinary acts of obedience. Further, grace was tied almost exclusively to the sacramental system of the church during this period. The stage was set for the cataclysmic changes that followed in the Reformation and Post-Reformation periods of the sixteenth and seventeenth centuries.

The Reformation and Post-Reformation Periods (1500–1750)

The Reformation largely set the agenda for the debates concerning grace that would emerge perennially in the ensuing centuries down to our own day. In one way or another, Augustine's theology of grace has continued to be the reference point for all the parties involved in these debates. The fundamental shift which took place at the time of the Reformation was in reference to the sacraments. The Reformers tied grace less to the sacraments, emphasizing more the *personal* quality of grace.

They also brought back the Augustinian doctrine of original sin, applying it to human reason and moving away from Aquinas' natural theology. Luther and Calvin moved back beyond the Scholastics in an effort to restore Augustinian concepts of sin and grace. Luther's key summary term for grace was *justification*. For Calvin it was *predestination*.

For Luther grace in its essence means that God justifies sinners. Calvin, a second generation reformer who would systematize the classic Reformation teachings, saw grace at its core as God's electing people without reference to foreseen merits or achievements, in other words, "unconditional election." The next logical step in the development of the Reformed tradition, then, would be to move to the doctrine of God, depicting his eternal decrees concerning all that is and all that transpires. In terms of the sixteenth and seventeenth centuries, however, the move toward the personal dimensions of grace and faith was all-important.

> The Reformation largely set the agenda for the debates concerning grace that would emerge perennially in the ensuing centuries down to our own day.

Salvation according to the Reformers was by grace alone (*sola gratia*) and through faith alone (*sola fide*). The Scriptures alone (*sola scriptura*) were considered the supreme authority of faith and life, and no intermediaries were needed, according to the Reformers, in establishing our saving relationship with God ("the priesthood of all believers"). This was no move, however, toward the radical individualism we have seen in American Christianity. The Reformers were churchmen to the core, and Luther himself never intended to divide the church, only to reform it. By the time of Calvin, however, the die had already been cast, and we have lived with the results of the Protestant/Catholic divide ever since.

Luther's pilgrimage was particularly poignant. His struggle to come to saving assurance, similar to Augustine before him and Wesley after him, has often been paradigmatic for many in subsequent generations. In effect, like Paul in his days as a zealous Pharisee, Luther sought a right relationship with God on the basis of his religious performance. And, as we all must learn sooner or later (as God brings us to the end of our resources), this is an impossible quest. The classic story of Luther's wresting with Romans 1:17 communicates the quintessential Lutheran concept of grace.

Luther would become enraged when he read the phrase, "the righteousness of God." This only reminded him of his failed efforts at trying to please and placate the peeved potentate he sought to serve. But one day he grasped the saving significance of this phrase: This righteous God was the *saving* God who gives us in Christ his righteousness as a gift we receive by faith. By grace alone! Through faith alone! And the Scriptures alone teach us this. The church, in the main, had lost this perspective. The gospel had been eclipsed by a new form of works-righteousness which came down to us through many ecclesiastical traditions, such as indulgences. Similar to Israel and Judah in ancient times, God's people had begun to *substitute* religious rites for personal faith. And Luther made the shattering discovery that he was, of all people, the most guilty of this error.

In his early years as a reformer (*ca.* 1515–19), Luther viewed justification more as process of becoming, of inward renewal. By the mid-1530s, however, perhaps through Melanchthon's influence, Luther taught *justification* as being declared righteous and *regeneration* as being transformed in the inner person, rightly delineating these biblical concepts. Ironically, the Council of Trent (1545–51) proved to be more Augustinian than Luther at this point, arguing that justification is a process of regeneration and renewal which changes both the inward and outward status of the person, as both event and process. Thus, a major misunderstanding emerged in which the church thought that Luther was saying that inward transformation and personal obedience were not important. If righteousness is only *imputed* and not *imparted* in justification, as Luther taught, then what is the true nature of justifying faith?

Luther would argue that the righteousness we receive in justification is *outside* of us, the "alien righteousness of Christ" (*iustitia Christi aliena*). The Council of Trent concluded that justification is a righteousness that is graciously infused or imparted to us and that we are justified on the basis of this internal righteousness. No, says Luther. Regeneration brings about spiritual transformation. Justification restores our relationship though a *gift* of God's righteousness. And sanctification continues in a lifelong transformation. Thus, in one sense, Luther and the Council of Trent were not that far apart, especially when seen in an Augustinian context. Luther, however, ever the careful exegete, had the stronger biblical basis. Recent dialogues across ecclesial boundaries have largely corroborated this conclusion.

But Luther had a true saving assurance. The Council of Trent saw the Reformers as presumptuous in teaching such a strong doctrine of assurance. The Protestant response was that such assurance was based solely on God's faithfulness to his promises. However, as we shall see, even the Protestants both then and now have never come to a complete consensus as to what constitutes such saving assurance. More specifically, how one deals with the nature of personal assurance and how one interprets apostasy are still a sticky issues, which must be addressed later in our treatment of the biblical doctrine of grace.

Calvin's great achievement was to write (at a very early age) a classical synthesis of the Reformed message in his *Institutes of the Christian Religion* (1559/60). But the brilliance of Calvin has become both a bane and blessing in present evangelical debates concerning grace. One can never fault Calvin's intentions to teach only what the Scriptures teach. His doctrinal works and commentaries are exemplary in that regard. What troubles many, however, is how Calvin's *followers*, particularly those who would seek to out reason (in good Aristotelian fashion) the Council of

Trent, would make Calvin's biblical interpretation of predestination the rational principle around which the entire faith is organized. That move, in the minds of many, simply distorts the biblical doctrine of grace. All Calvin himself was doing was simply to present the whole counsel of Scripture. Thus, in the second half of the *Institutes*, in his teachings on the doctrines of salvation, Calvin includes a discussion of election and predestination. Even apart from the sterile rationalism of some forms of extreme Calvinism, some are still troubled by the biblical theology Calvin sets forth here.

For Calvin, predestination is absolute, particular, and double in nature. Predestination is absolute, resting solely on God's immutable will, not on divine foreknowledge of human contingencies. It is particular, in that it pertains to *individuals*, and Christ dies only for those elect individuals. And it is double in nature: Some are ordained to eternal life (to the praise of God's mercy), and others are ordained to eternal damnation (to the praise of God's justice).

Evangelicals have had a love/hate relationship with Calvin. To some, Calvin's theology is the epitome of Christian doctrine and his mind one of the most brilliant in Christian history. Even the Neoorthodox giant, Karl Barth, stood in awe of Calvin. To others, Calvin is a demon in the worst sense of that term—and Calvin's God as well! Surely the truth lies somewhere between these extremes. Without doubt, Calvin raised most of the key issues with which we still wrestle today.[9] Which observation brings us to the modern (and now postmodern) era in which we live.

The Modern Period *(1750–Present)*

The Enlightenment of the eighteenth century brought with it (in Kantian fashion) the enthronement of human reason over divine revelation. Voltaire and Rousseau, for example, would vigorously oppose the doctrine of original sin—and, therefore, the need of divine grace—as

---

[9] For an engaging and informative treatment of Calvin as well as the other Protestant divines see Timothy George's *Theology of the Reformers* (Nashville: Broadman Press, 1988).

encouraging pessimism and impeding social and political growth. Unfortunately, this Enlightenment rationalism crept into Christian theology as well. In fact, in large measure the history of Christian theology since then has been the history of the church's struggle against, and too often embracing of, Enlightenment rubrics. Modernistic theology capitulated to the Enlightenment, while postmodern theology seems to have learned the hard lessons of the limits of human reason and technology, but to have capitulated to relativism. The "Father of Modern (Liberal) Theology," F. D. E. Schleiermacher (1768–1834), in many ways saw the issues quite clearly.

If we can no longer accept the inspiration and trustworthiness of the Scriptures in traditional terms, which Schleiermacher assumed we could not, then one way to salvage the faith is to appeal to our *experience* of God's grace. Schleiermacher founded his whole system of theology on this approach, appealing to three pillars of our faith: (1) dependence upon God, (2) awareness of sin and guilt, and (3) the transforming power of grace. Schleiermacher was attempting to have his cake and eat it too. He tried to hold to his pietistic roots while at the same time accepting the naturalistic and pluralistic humanism of his day. Thus, one hears the overtones of the old heretic Pelagius in Schleiermacher's writings! The world wars exploded such optimism, however, and Neoorthodox theologians such as Karl Barth (1886–1968), Emil Brunner (1889–1966), and Reinhold Neibuhr (1892–1971) sought to recover the Augustinian doctrine of sin and grace. Barth's theology of grace in particular warrants notice.

When Barth shifted from preaching the Enlightenment liberalism he had imbibed in seminary to the exposition of Scripture, he inadvertently started a theological revolution. It all began with the publication of his commentary on the book of Romans. Barth had rediscovered grace! His was a Reformed, Calvinistic theology which taught a strong view of sin, the centrality of Christ, and a dynamic view of grace. Unfortunately, Barth's journey back to the Bible was never completed, and he went far beyond the Scriptures in his depiction of a radical triumph of grace resulting in the salvation of *all* persons (universalism). But Barth was always slippery on this issue. My theological mentor, Dale Moody, knew Barth well and tried to corner him on the subject. "Dr. Barth," Moody asked, "do you believe God is going to save everyone?" Barth smiled, winked, and said, "You wouldn't get mad if he did, would you?" Even in some evangelical circles today we are still plagued with universalism.

In the main, however, evangelicals of all stripes—Reformed, Arminian, Pentecostal, charismatic, and so on—have remained faithful to the Christian consensus that "by grace you have been saved through faith, and this is not your own doing; it is the gift of God—not the result of works, so that no one may boast" (Eph. 2:8–9). But when we get into the finer points of discussion of this soteriology, the debates inevitably heat up! And that, in part, is the purpose of this study. What *do* the Scriptures teach in relation to grace? This would seem to be the next step we should take in our exploration of God's amazing grace.

Chapter Four:
Grace in Scripture

The Hebrew Bible

WE ENCOUNTER THE GRACE OF GOD in the very opening words of the Bible. The majestic account of creation in Genesis 1 and 2 provides our first siting of common grace, as a good God makes a good universe and humankind in his own image. He blesses his creation and cares for it through his human regents. Already we see God ordering, governing, and preserving all that he has made. This common grace gives way to special, saving grace in the third chapter. In the midst of judgment, in what scholars have often called the *Protoevangelium*, the first announcement of the gospel of grace is made: "I will put enmity between you and the woman, and between your offspring and hers; he will strike your head, and you will strike his heal" (Gen. 3:15).

Jesus Christ, "born of a woman" (Gal. 4:4), born of a virgin (Matt. 1:23/Isa. 7:14), would decisively deal with this enmity between the serpent and humanity and defeat the evil one through the cross and the resurrection. Henri Blocher sees a further note of grace in God's clothing the primal couple in animal skins, covering their sin and degradation (Gen. 3:21).[1] In addition, we should note a crucial dimension of the biblical doctrine of grace: God's redeeming love does not eradicate his holy judgment. Most of the distortions of grace we encounter err at just this point—either in universalism or in a diluted doctrine of atonement. Grace is an expression of God's *holy* love. The stories of Cain, Noah, and the Tower of Babel which follow also develop this theme of grace amidst judgment.

---
[1] Henri Blocher, *In the Beginning*, trans. David G. Preston (Downers Grove, Ill.: InterVarsity Press, 1984), 191.

The avalanche which follows the fall in Eden begins with a fratricide (Gen. 4:1–16). The Lord had already graciously warned Cain of the sin "lurking at the door" (v. 7), but he pays no heed. When confronted with the Lord's question, "Where is Abel your brother?" Cain is impudent: "How should I know? Am I his babysitter?" (Gen. 4:9, The Message). God's judgment is swift and certain, but with a note of grace: a mark of protection to avert Cain's being killed in his fugitive wanderings. But things only get worse.

People had become so wicked by Noah's day that "every inclination of the thoughts of their hearts was only evil continually" (Gen. 6:5). The Lord was "grieved" that he had ever made us and "his heart was filled with pain" (v. 6 NIV[1984]). Then comes the hint of divine grace in the midst of judgment: "But Noah found grace in the eyes of the Lord" (v. 8 NKJV). Here we have the first occurrence of an important Hebrew term for grace, *chen* (generally translated as "favor" in most modern versions).

The Bible of the early church was a Greek translation of the Hebrew Scriptures, which we know as the Septuagint. Since it is the version most often quoted by the New Testament writers, it is important to note that *chen* is consistently translated as *charis*, "grace," in the Septuagint and serves as an important background term for the New Testament doctrine of grace (particularly in Paul). The term, used some sixty-one times in the Hebrew Bible, refers to a superior one freely stooping to help an inferior one, whether on the human level or in the divine-human encounter. We see divine favor being given not only to Noah (Gen. 6:8), but also to Abraham (Gen. 8:3), Moses (Ex. 33:12–13; 34:9), Gideon (Judg. 6:17), and David (2 Sam. 15:25). God graciously elects leaders to carry out his redemptive plans. At the end of the age, the Lord says, "I will pour out on the house of David and on the inhabitants of Jerusalem, the Spirit of grace [*chen*] and of supplication, so that they will look on Me whom they have pierced; … [and] mourn" (Zech. 12:10 NASB; see John 19:37). Thus, Israel will finally recognize her Messiah, and God's plan of grace for both Jew and Gentile will be culminated.

Judgment and grace are found together in Jeremiah's prophecies as well. After twenty-nine chapters of judgment announcements, the Book of Consolation (30:1–33:26) shockingly appears, heralding the ultimate restoration of Israel and Judah—all this being proclaimed *the year before Nebuchadnezzar razed the city of Jerusalem and hauled off God's people into exile in Babylon!* The opening verses of chapter 31 contain three of the key Hebrew terms which serve as a backdrop for the New Testament's teachings on grace (Jer. 31:1–3):

> At that time, says the Lord, I will be the God of all the families
> of Israel, and they shall be my people.
> Thus says the Lord:
> The people who survived the sword
>   found grace [chen] in the wilderness;
> when Israel sought for rest,
>   the Lord appeared to him from far away.
> I have loved you with an everlasting love [ahabah];
>   therefore, I have continued my faithfulness [chesed] to you.

Chen we have already looked at. *Ahabah*, "love," summarizes the entire Bible, which is composed of two "Testaments of Love."[2] And *chesed*—variously rendered "lovingkindness," "steadfast love," "covenant love," or simply "love"—may be the most important Hebrew word behind the New Testament term *charis*, "grace." In addition, this same chapter contains the one and only use of the phrase, "new covenant" (vv. 31–34; see Heb. 8:8–12; 10:16–17), which points forward to the good news of Jesus Christ and provides the title for our Scriptures as the New Testament (Covenant)!

Moses reminded the children of Israel, as they were poised to enter the promised land, that it was because of God's love (*ahabah*) alone that they were his people. It had nothing to do with any merit on their part:

> It was not because you were more numerous than any other
> people that the Lord set his heart on you and chose you—for you
> were the fewest of all peoples. It was because the Lord loved you

---

[2] See Leon Morris, *Testaments of Love: A Study of Love in the Bible* (Grand Rapids, Mich.: Eerdmans, 1981).

and kept the oath that he swore to your ancestors, that the Lord has brought you out with a mighty hand, and redeemed you from the house of slavery, from the hand of Pharaoh king of Egypt (Deut. 7:7–8).

Moses goes on to mention the "covenant loyalty" (*chesed*) of Israel's "faithful God" (v. 8). Grace as God's undeserved love, mercy, and deliverance could not be more evident.

Chesed occurs some 250 times in the Hebrew Bible and is translated as *eleos*, "mercy," in the Septuagint. It is virtually synonymous with grace and salvation in terms of the merciful attitude and action of God toward undeserving humanity that it expresses. For example, Psalm 119:41, utilizing a Hebrew parallelism in which the second line further defines or re-expresses the first line, says:

> Let your *steadfast love* [*chesed*] come to me, O Lord,
> Your *salvation* according to your promise.

Having witnessed the destruction of Jerusalem, Jeremiah (or whoever wrote Lamentations), held out the hope of God's saving mercy:

> But this I call to mind,
> and therefore I have hope:
> The steadfast love [*chesed*] of the Lord never ceases,
> his mercies never come to an end;
> they are new every morning;
> great is your faithfulness (Lam. 3:21–23).

Two other related terms round out our list: *channun*, "gracious," and *chanan*, "to be gracious." And perhaps the best summary passage to put all these together would be the words that the Lord himself spoke to Moses on Mount Sinai.

Yahweh was ready to break out in judgment against the children of Israel, but Moses interceded (Ex. 32). Then, because of the favor Moses has with the Lord as his chosen leader, God reveals himself in a majestic way to Moses and renews the covenant (Ex. 33–34). His majestic words to Moses during that revelation on Mount Sinai became an Apostles' Creed, as it were, for God's people:

> The LORD, the LORD,
> a God merciful and gracious,
> slow to anger,
> and abounding in steadfast love and faithfulness… (Ex. 34:6).

Here we have what my mentor, Dale Moody, called the Five Points of Yahwism, referring to God's mercy, grace, patience, kindness, and faithfulness.[3] These revelatory words to Moses became central to Israel's faith (Ex. 34:6-7; see Num. 14:18; Neh. 9:17, 31; Pss. 86:15; 103:8; 145:8; Jer. 32:18; Joel 2:13; Jon. 4:2; Nah.1:3; also, Ex. 20:5-6 and Deut. 5:9, 10). By his own self-attestation, God is a God of mercy and grace, and the rich language of the Hebrew Scriptures reflects this as well.

Returning to the primeval history of the first eleven chapters of Genesis, we were looking at Noah on the eve of the flood. Noah had found grace, or favor, with the Lord (Gen. 6:8). God was still going to judge the world, but he kept a remnant, Noah's family, to repopulate the planet. In addition, the Lord gave another emblem of grace in the rainbow of promise, the sign of a covenant that God would never again destroy the world through a flood (Gen. 9:8-19).

The primeval prologue culminates with the final event of the avalanche of sin that ensued from the fall of the first couple: the Tower of Babel (Gen. 11:1-9). Here is sinful, secular humanity shaking its fist in God's face and defying his sovereignty. God's judgment will descend yet again in response to human rebellion. But this is also a turning point in the Genesis narrative. From chapter 12 onward—through the rest of the Scriptures, in fact!—we have the story of God's gracious plan of redemption, beginning with the call of Abram (Gen. 12). Reading the first eleven chapters of Genesis leaves us with a sense of despair. Humanity is incorrigible, hopeless, continually under divine judgment.

---

[3] Dale Moody, *The Word of Truth* (Grand Rapids, Mich.: Eerdmans, 1981), 104.

But then comes grace: God elects Abram for a saving mission which will ultimately encompass the totality of humankind.[4]

One wonders whether the Tower of Babel might be paradigmatic for every generation. Most certainly, it applies to our present-day urbanized, secularized world. As Jacques Ellul has argued, the city became the ultimate symbol of humanity's rebellion against God. Thus, God chose to confuse their languages in the land of Shinar, where they were building their godless city. It was, in the final analysis, a gracious move on God's apart, averting their deadly independence. At the end of the age, paradise is restored with God's gracious gift of a city, the new Jerusalem coming down out of heaven![5] Some students of Luke have even argued that Pentecost, another language miracle, was God's reversal of Babel. Now all peoples can be united in the kingdom of God through the gospel of Christ.[6]

What has become readily apparent already in this brief survey of the Old Testament is that a narrative approach to the Scriptures yields much more insight into God's amazing grace than simple word studies. The stories of Abraham, Isaac, Jacob, Joseph, Ruth, Hannah, Samuel, David, Solomon, Isaiah, Jeremiah, Ezekiel, Daniel, Hosea, Jonah, and many others are replete with teachings on divine grace in all its dimensions. Jesus himself used narrative more often than not in his teachings. It is becoming increasingly apparent that the old rubric that doctrine must be derived primarily from the didactic portions is a grossly distorted hermeneutic. One last example will suffice to illustrate this principle.

Jacob was a cheater, a liar, and a con-man. Yet God chose him to inherit his fathers' promised blessings as divinely chosen vessels. Twice the Lord intervened in Jacob's life when he was fleeing as a fugitive from those he had cheated. The first time, Jacob found himself in the wilderness,

---

[4] See Gerhard von Rad, *Genesis*, trans. J. H. Marks, OTL, 2nd ed. (Philadelphia: Westminster, 1972), 153.
[5] See Jacques Ellul, *The Meaning of the City* (Grand Rapids, Mich.: Eerdmans, 1970).
[6] The following resources were helpful in developing this section: Bruce Demarest, *The Cross and Salvation*, Foundations of Evangelical Theology (Wheaton, Ill.: Crossway, 1997), 70–72; J. I. Packer, *God's Words: Studies of Key Bible Themes* (Grand Rapids, Mich.: Baker, 1981), 96–97; relevant study notes in: *NIV Study Bible* (Grand Rapids, Mich.: Zondervan, 2002) and *Ryrie Study Bible*, expanded ed. (Chicago: Moody Press, 1995).

heading toward Haran and away from his brother Esau. The Lord arrests him with a startling revelation in a dream of a stairway to heaven. Instead of berating Jacob for his conniving ways, the Lord announces his gracious, saving plans for both Jacob and his descendants (Gen. 28:10–22). The second time, decades later, Jacob is fleeing Laban. It was the night before he was to meet Esau. In one of the strangest encounters with God ever recorded, Jacob again experiences the grace of God. He found himself wrestling with God, and he would emerge a changed man with a new name. His name from now on, it was announced, would be Israel, he who struggles with God (Gen. 32:22–32). This cherished name, for millions of people of faith, is "a name that puts the final seal of God's grace on him. Jacob the cheat becomes the namesake of God's chosen people, the 'Israelites.'"[7]

> *Jacob was a cheater, a liar, and a con-man. Yet God chose him to inherit his fathers' promised blessings as divinely chosen vessels.*

But the story doesn't end there. Centuries later, the apostle Paul, whose own life had been transformed, would point back to Jacob's experience to illustrate the nature of God's "unfair" grace. Quoting Malachi 1:1–3—"I have loved Jacob, but I have hated Esau"—Paul reminds us that God's electing grace has nothing to do with our having "done anything good or bad" (Rom. 9:10–13). Paul was haunted by his own people's having rejected their Messiah. Had God's plan of redemption failed, since it was patently clear that "not all Israelites truly belong to Israel, and not all of Abraham's children are his true descendants" (Rom. 9:1–6)? The fault of their unbelief could certainly not be laid at God's door. And besides that, God's gracious plans for Israel were not yet completed (Rom. 9–11)!

Malachi, many centuries after Jacob, was writing about God's judgment upon the Edomites (the descendants of Esau) and God's blessings

---

[7] *The NIV Student Bible*, rev. ed. (Grand Rapids, Mich.: Zondervan, 2002), 38.

upon the Israelites (the descendants of Jacob)—again, judgment and grace coming together. But Paul would have us never lose sight of the *individual*, Jacob. We are as undeserving of God's love as Jacob himself—or any of his descendants.

The New Testament

The term for grace in the New Testament is *charis*. It is found 155 times, approximately 100 of which are in Paul's letters.[8] Therefore, we will give special attention to Paul's use of this term. In addition, there are a number of different ways *charis* may be rendered, according to the context. Paul's Colossians epistle provides us with good examples. Toward the end of his letter, the apostle exhorts his readers, "Let your speech always be gracious, seasoned with salt, so that you may know how you ought to answer everyone" (4:6). A strictly literal rendering of Paul's words could be, "Let your speech *(logos)* always be with grace *(charis)*, seasoned with salt, so that you may know how to answer everyone." In other words, sometimes grace means *graciousness*. Our conversation should be gracious and attractive, with wit and wisdom. Earlier, Paul had written, "with gratitude in your hearts sing psalms, hymns, and spiritual songs to God" (Col. 3:16)—literally, "with *grace* in your hearts." So grace can simply signify gratitude. In the thanksgiving portion of his letter, Paul uses grace in the theological sense of the term. He describes the dynamic spread of the gospel among the Colossians as their comprehending "the grace of God" (Col. 1:7). And Paul begins and ends his epistle by wishing them God's grace (1:2; 4:18). There is much more to be said about grace in Pauline theology, but the point being made is obvious. Further, we see again that merely doing a word study truncates our understanding of grace in the New Testament. Our goal in this chapter will be to obtain a grasp of the overall concept of grace in the New Testament, leaving additional details and theological discussion for subsequent chapters.

---

[8] Demarest, *The Cross and Salvation*, 72.

Luke-Acts

Rather arbitrarily, I would like to begin with one of my favorite New Testament theologians: Luke. Contemporary New Testament scholarship has impressed upon us the essential insight that each New Testament writer should be allowed to speak for himself. Greater precision is attained in this manner than by merely "homogenizing" the Bible's teachings. Luke was quite an impressive individual: medical doctor, missionary, historian, and *theologian*.[9] And he demonstrated an originality in his use of the term *grace*.[10]

Having been a missionary companion of Paul, Luke may have developed a similar charismology (doctrine of grace) precisely because they both were privileged to witness firsthand the workings of God's grace in the spread of the gospel. In addition, Luke's pneumatology (doctrine of the Spirit) looms large throughout his two-volume work. And, as with Paul, there appears to be a strong correlation between grace and the Spirit. One unmistakable way to gain access to this insight is to compare the infancy narratives in the first two chapters of the gospel with the opening chapters of the Acts narratives.[11]

Obviously, Luke emphasizes the role of the Holy Spirit in both contexts, but too often the *grace* of God is overlooked. Two summary statements characterize Jesus' boyhood: "And the child grew and became strong; he was filled with wisdom, and the grace of God was upon him" (Luke 2:40 TNIV); "And as Jesus grew up, he increased in wisdom and in favor [*charis*] with God and people" (Luke 2:52 TNIV). In the former, Luke uses *charis* in the more dynamic, pneumatological sense. In the latter, the more straightforward significance of "favor" seems evident. A comparison with Acts corroborates this observation.

Luke's summary statement in Acts 4:32–35 includes the words, "and great grace was upon them all"—both the apostles, who with "great

---
[9] See I. Howard Marshall, *Luke: Historian and Theologian* (Grand Rapids, Mich.: Zondervan, 1970).
[10] See James Moffatt, *Grace in the New Testament* (London: Hodder & Stoughton, 1931).
[11] See George T. Montague, *The Holy Spirit: Growth of a Biblical Tradition* (New York: Paulist Press, 1976), 264–65.

power ... gave their testimony to the resurrection of the Lord Jesus," and the people, who freely shared their possessions with one another. As the gospel continued to spread, Barnabas was able to observe firsthand "the grace of God" at Antioch (Acts 11:23). What did he *see* that caused him to rejoice? They had received the gospel. They had received the Lord. And Barnabas "exhorted them all to remain faithful to the Lord with steadfast devotion" (v. 23). Truly this was evidence of the "hand of the Lord" (Acts 11:21). Again, we see a dynamic view of grace here. More specifically, Barnabas, "a good man, full of the Holy Spirit and faith" (v. 24), saw it!

Later, Paul and Barnabas would see a similar breakthrough in Pisidian Antioch and would exhort the new believers there "to continue in the grace of God" (Acts 13:43). At Iconium, even in the face of staunch resistance, Paul and Barnabas spoke "boldly for the Lord, who confirmed the message [*logos*] of his grace by enabling them to do miraculous signs and wonders" (Acts 14:3 TNIV). Here the emphasis is on the *content* of the faith, the gospel, which is summarized in the one word *grace*. But we should also take note of the accompanying "signs and wonders," which confirmed their message. These works of power were also evidence of the grace of God upon the apostles (compare again Acts 4:33). Having completed the work of their first missionary journey, Paul and Barnabas returned to Antioch, "where they had been commended to the grace of God for the work [or committed in the grace of God to the work (NRSV note)] that they had completed" (Acts 14:26). How had they been thus commended or committed? Acts 13:1–3 describes the event, which included worshipping, fasting, prayer, prophecy ("the Holy Spirit said"), and the laying on of hands—again, a dynamic understanding of grace.

The most dangerous challenge to the message of grace would arise from *within* the church itself. Paul and Barnabas had remained with the disciples at Antioch for an extended period of time, when "certain individuals came down from Judea and were teaching the brothers, 'Unless you are circumcised according to the custom of Moses, you cannot be saved'" (Acts 14:28–15:1). Predictably, "Paul and Barnabas had no small dissension and debate with them" (Acts 15:2). The two apostles, along with some others, were sent to Jerusalem to bring the question to the apostles and elders there. On the way, as they passed through Phoenicia and Samaria, they reported the Gentiles' conversions and "brought great joy to all the believers" (v. 3). Here is another leitmotif in Luke's symphony of grace: Grace (*charis*) brings joy (*chara*). Both words are from the same root (*char*). The gospel of Luke and the book of Acts are filled with joy and rejoicing at the spread of the gospel of grace.[12] And the surest way to lose the freedom and joy of salvation is to move away from grace into a subtle, or not so subtle, legalism. This was precisely what the sect of the Pharisees in Jerusalem were trying to foist upon the infant church (v. 5).

> *The surest way to lose the freedom and joy of salvation is to move away from grace into a subtle, or not so subtle, legalism.*

In typical fashion, Peter spoke up first at the council meeting, concluding "we believe that we will be saved through the grace of the Lord Jesus" and arguing against "a yoke that neither our ancestors nor we have been able to bear" (vv. 10–11). How was this saving grace manifested? God, "who knows the human heart," had given them (the Gentiles) his Holy Spirit and cleansed their hearts by faith (vv. 8–9). Then Paul and Barnabas "told of all the signs and wonders that God had done through them among the Gentiles" (v. 12). Finally, James, the Lord's brother, wrapped it up and suggested a course of action (vv. 13–21). The believers "rejoiced" (again, the note of joy) when they received the letter from the council (v. 31).

---

[12] See William G. Morrice, *Joy in the New Testament* (Greenwood, S.C.: The Attic Press, 1984), ch. 14 "The Gospel of Joy and Its Sequel—Luke and Acts," 91–99 for a thorough and edifying study of this motif. See also, William Barclay, *Flesh and Spirit* (Nashville: Abingdon, 1962), 76–83.

Paul's second missionary journey was also marked by grace. He was commended again "to the grace of the Lord" before he set out, having chosen Silas to accompany him (Acts 15:40). Unfortunately, there may have been some "ungrace," as Philip Yancey would call it, involved in Paul's rejection of John Mark and separation from Barnabas (vv. 37–39). Acts contains three other references to grace which should be noted.

Apollos had been sent from Ephesus to Achaia. "On his arrival he greatly helped those who *through grace had become believers*" (Acts 18:27). It is through grace—and only through grace—that anyone ever becomes a believer. This teaching is unmistakable in the New Testament and must be kept in mind in the Calvinism/Arminianism debates that inevitably surface.

The culmination of Luke's teachings on grace is found in Paul's words to the Ephesian elders: (1) "I don't care about my own life. The most important thing is that I complete my mission, the work that the Lord Jesus gave me—to tell people the Good News about God's grace" (Acts 20:24 NCV); (2) "And now I commend you to God and to the message of his grace, a message that is able to build you up and to give you the inheritance among all who are sanctified"

> It is through grace and only through grace that anyone ever becomes a believer.

(Acts 20:32). The first statement should be *our* life mission as well. And the second statement is the prescription for just about everything that is crippling the present-day church. The message of grace alone will build up the church. And it is perhaps the most neglected teaching of all. How many of us, for example, can give a coherent statement of the gospel? How many others of us are caught on a performance treadmill, trying to win God's favor? May God increase the tribes of the Philip Yanceys and Brennan Mannings of this world, who so powerfully communicate this liberating message of the grace of God.[13]

John

I had the privilege of viewing the film *The Gospel of John* when it was first released to theaters nationwide. Never have I been more impacted by a film. The film presents John's gospel word for word from the *Good News Bible*. I happened to be writing this very chapter when I saw the film. Grace pervades almost every frame! As I reflected on this outstanding visual presentation, it struck me that virtually every chapter of the gospel of John contains something related to the biblical doctrine of grace. Ironically, the term *grace* is used only four times, all found in the prologue (John 1:14, 16–17), but the concept "runs through his whole Gospel."[14]

Readers in John's day would have been familiar with the practice and purpose of placing a prologue at the beginning of a work. Homer's *Iliad* and *Odyssey*, both of which had carefully crafted prologues, were popular works during that time. A prologue sets the tone and introduces the major themes of the work, providing important background information.[15] Certainly John's majestic prologue (John 1:1–18) achieves these ends. Thus, one of the themes we should be alerted to throughout his gospel will be that of grace.

Verses 1–13 all lead up to the great event described in verse 14: "And the Word became flesh." Many of John's readers (those who espoused docetism) would be horrified by these words: Material flesh, in their view, is inherently evil![16] But for the Christian faith nothing could be more central. In our own day, especially in conservative circles, we still struggle with this Gnostic heresy which cannot embrace Christ's

---

[13] See, for example, Philip Yancey, *What's So Amazing About Grace?* (Grand Rapids, Mich.: Zondervan, 1997) and Brennan Manning, *The Ragamuffin Gospel* (Sisters, Oregon: Multnomah, 1990).
[14] Leon Morris, *Jesus Is the Christ: Studies in the Theology of John* (Grand Rapids, Mich.: Eerdmans, 1989), 94.
[15] Philip W. Comfort and Wendell C. Hawley, *Opening the Gospel of John* (Wheaton, Ill.: Tyndale, 1994), 1.
[16] F. F. Bruce, *The Gospel of John* (Grand Rapids, Mich.: Eerdmans, 1983), 39.

full humanity. Thus, the rendering of these words found in the *Good News Bible* is even more helpful: "The Word became a human being." But there is more: "And the Word became flesh and dwelt among us" (ESV). The word "dwelt" hearkens back to the Shekinah glory in the Tabernacle. God has pitched his tent among us! He has moved into the neighborhood! That is a glorious truth!

John continues with these words: "and we have seen his glory, glory as of the only Son from the Father, full of grace and truth" (ESV). Another glorious Old Testament event is evoked with these additional words. Moses had asked the Lord permission to see his glory, and the Lord announced that he was going to make all his goodness pass before him (Ex. 33:18–19). The Lord's proclamation during that glorious revelation included these descriptive words: "abounding in steadfast love and faithfulness" (Ex. 34:6). Put the two phrases side by side. Grace (*charis*) and truth (*aletheia*)/steadfast love (*chesed*) and faithfulness (*emet*). Now we see how the testaments correlate. *Charis* corresponds to *chesed* and so forth. God's glory is God's goodness. The God of glory is the God of grace who dwells among us. John, therefore, sees God's glory in the Incarnate Word who goes to the cross for us. Verse 15 is parenthetical, and verse 16 continues John's description of the Logos. "And from his fullness we have all received grace upon grace" (ESV). From Christ's fullness we experience wave after wave of the inexhaustible ocean of God's grace.

> The God of glory is the God of grace who dwells among us.

Then John mentions Moses explicitly: "For the law was given though Moses; grace and truth came through Jesus Christ" (v. 17 ESV). We have already seen grace in the revelation to Moses, but now something new and radical has happened. "Here, then, as in Paul's writings, Christ displaces the law of Moses as the focus of divine revelation and the way to life."[17] Now grace stands before us incarnate, in person! That is what the gospel of John is all about, and that is why it is the book we often start with in our Christian pilgrimage.

Instead of Torah and Temple, John argues, our focus should now be on the Incarnate Lord himself. Immediately, we see John the Baptist drawing attention to Jesus: "Here is the Lamb of God who takes away the sin of the world!" (John 1:29). John depicts Jesus as the Lamb of God, the Baptizer in the Holy Spirit, and the Son of God (John 1:29–34). The entire gospel is bracketed in these categories. In the crucifixion narrative, John highlights the blood and water that issue from our Savior's side (John 19:34–35). *Blood*: "Here is the Lamb of God"; *Water*: "[This is] the one who baptizes in the Holy Spirit." And John's declared purpose is that we believe that Jesus is the Messiah, the Son of God, and thereby have life in his name (John 20:31). Grace in John entails atonement through the blood of Christ and eternal life through his Spirit. He alone can give the water of eternal life.

> Now grace stands before us incarnate, in person!

Other selected passages in John bear witness to divine grace. For example, we see grace in Jesus' calling Andrew and Peter (1:35–42) and Philip and Nathanael (1:43–51). Jesus' words to Nathanael are particularly noteworthy: "Very truly, I tell you, you will see heaven opened and the angels of God ascending and descending upon the Son of Man" (v. 51). These words echo, of course, Jacob's gracious encounter with the Lord (Gen. 28:12). Jesus uses the metaphor of the mysterious wind to communicate the miracle of new birth, regenerational grace, to Nicodemus (John 3:1–20), a passage which contains perhaps the best known scripture on earth: John 3:16. Jesus uses the metaphor of water to communicate the same reality of eternal life to the Samaritan woman at Jacob's well in Sychar (John 4:1–42). Later Jesus uses the same metaphor at the Jerusalem festival to offer his saving grace to the masses (John 7:37–39).

---

[17] Bruce, *The Gospel of John*, 43.

The memorable and well known story about the woman caught in adultery is a classic grace narrative (John 8:2-11). And Jesus, as the good shepherd, graciously cares for and protects those whom God has given him (John 10:1-18). Then, Jesus' washing of the disciples' feet communicates the humble grace of the Master toward his own in an unforgettable way (John 13:1-20). It also reminds us of the grace we are to show toward one another. In the upper room discourse (John 14-16) and in Jesus' high priestly prayer (John 17) we have further instruction and example concerning the workings of grace in our lives through the Holy Spirit. John's passion narrative (John 18-20), of course, is grace writ large. Finally, John's concluding chapter (John 21) portrays Jesus' restoration of Peter. If anyone understood the grace, mercy, and patience of the Lord, it was Simon Peter! A similar survey could be given for each of the Synoptic gospels (Matthew, Mark, and Luke), but perhaps the best way to get at the heart of the teaching of grace in these gospels would be to take a quick glance at Jesus' parables.

The Parables of Jesus

Jesus' use of parables set him apart. A simple story remains with the hearer and, upon reflection, teaches volumes. Without using the word *grace*, these powerful teachings nevertheless effectively communicated grace and other kingdom realities. The parable of the sower—perhaps better titled the parable of the soils, since that is its emphasis—serves as an excellent example (Matt. 13:1-9, 18-23; Mark 4:1-9, 13-20; Luke 8:4-8, 11-15). This is one parable in which Jesus himself provides his dominical interpretation. And he does so, in contrast to a waning scholarly consensus which strictly allows only one point per parable, in an *allegorical* fashion, making several points.[18] Jesus does not comment on the identity of the sower, but the implied reference is to the God of the kingdom himself. We need to notice both the seed and the soils.

---

[18] Craig L. Blomberg is a helpful guide in this regard: *Interpreting the Parables* (Downers Grove, Ill.: InterVarsity Press, 1990).

The seed, Jesus says explicitly, is "the word" (Mark 4:4), "the word of God" (Luke 8:11), or "the word of the kingdom" (Matt. 13:19). "The sowing of the seed is the pronouncement of God's provision of grace. But the soils focus on the human response, which is clearly varied."[19] This parable inevitably raises, therefore, the mystery of the relation between divine sovereignty and human freedom. More specifically, it provokes the question as to whether God's grace can be resisted. Much more will be said concerning these questions later. At the very least, the parable points to the reality anyone faces in pastoral and evangelistic ministries: People respond in different ways to the gospel of grace and most often for mysterious reasons beyond our understanding.

The good soil represents "the ones who, when they hear the word, hold it fast in an honest and good heart, and bear fruit with patient endurance" (Luke 8:15). But that is only one of four responses to the gospel. The seed also falls on the path, pointing to "those who have heard; then the devil comes and takes away the word from their hearts, so that they may not believe and be saved" (Luke 8:12). Most interpreters have few difficulties with these two soils. The other two soils are more troubling. What about the ones on the rocky ground? "When they hear the word, they immediately receive it with joy. But they have no root, and endure only for a while; then, when trouble or persecution arises on account of the word, immediately they fall away" (Mark 4:16–17). Clearly, the response is superficial in these cases, with no enduring faith. But the third soil haunts us American believers even more. The seed that fell among the thorns, Jesus said, points to those who are "choked by the cares and riches and pleasures of life, and their fruit does not mature" (Luke 8:14). Is this not a description of too large a segment of the American church? Especially, in Luke's account do we perceive Jesus' teaching on the importance of perseverance, endurance, and maturity. These examples of human responses to grace raise two additional crucial issues: apostasy and assurance. What does it mean

---

[19] Donald Guthrie, *New Testament Theology* (Downers Grove, Ill.: InterVarsity Press, 1981), 603–04.

to fall away? And what is the basis of a true assurance of faith? These questions deserve the extended analysis they will receive in a later chapter. Thomas R. Schreiner and Ardel B. Caneday observe that this parable "is like a mirror. It reflects how we hear the gospel. It does its work as we hear it, for it rebukes the disingenuous and assures those who bear fruit with perseverance."[20]

Two realities to contemplate: seed and soils—God's provision of grace and our response. Is this a *monergistic* reality in which God does everything, and we are merely passive recipients? Or is this a *synergistic* reality in which there is a flowing together of divine and human activity? These questions will certainly emerge again for our exploration. But either way we go, we must ultimately conclude that *God* does the saving, not us. He is the sower, and it is his kingdom. Can we have confidence that God will accomplish his plans and finish what he has started? The parables of the mustard seed and the yeast answer this concern incontrovertibly.

God's kingdom entails *growth*. And both Matthew and Luke include these dual parables of our Lord concerning the mustard seed and yeast to point to this reality (Matt. 13:31–33; Luke 13:18–21; see also Mark 4:30–32). Can we be confident that God will accomplish his saving purposes? Jesus says yes and uses two stark contrasts to make his point. The kingdom starts small, like a tiny mustard seed or a small portion of yeast. But it grows large, like a tree or a large batch of dough. And this growth is inexorable. "Their meaning is that out of the most insignificant beginnings, invisible to the human eye, God creates his mighty Kingdom, which embraces all the peoples of the world."[21] As Donald Guthrie says of the parable of the yeast, "[it] focuses on the invisible yet certain operation of grace."[22] Just as Paul was confident that God would finish what he had started among the Philippians (Phil. 1:6), so we can be confident God will finish his saving work in our own lives. This as-

---

[20] Thomas R. Schreiner and Ardel B. Caneday, *The Race Set Before Us: A Biblical Theology of Perseverance & Assurance* (Downers Grove, Ill.: InterVarsity Press, 2001), 221–22.

[21] Joachim Jeremias, *The Parables of Jesus* (New York: Scribner's, 1972), 149.

[22] Guthrie, *New Testament Theology*, 604.

surance is sometimes called *preserving grace* by the theologians. In this same context, Matthew adds two additional parables, reminding us of the grace-basis of the entire reality of our lives under God's saving reign.

The parables of the hidden treasure and the pearl remind us of how priceless God's gift of the kingdom is:

> The kingdom of heaven is like treasure hidden in a field, which someone found and hid; then in his joy he goes and sells all that he has and buys that field.
> Again, the kingdom of heaven is like a merchant in search of fine pearls; on finding one pearl of great value, he went and sold all that he had and bought it (Matt. 13:44–46).

Notice the sacrifice, selling all that they had, but notice also the joy (v. 44). But most important of all, notice the infinite value of God's kingdom. Salvation is free but costly. "But we do not purchase the kingdom; quite the contrary, God rules entirely by grace."[23] Perhaps missionaries best exemplify this truth. We are amazed at the sacrifices they make to take the message of grace to the nations. Most of the time, they seem oblivious to the sacrifice involved in their joyous, energetic service. Their lives are simplified, focused, and serene. *All* of our lives would be so if we would simply cooperate with God's grace at work in our lives. When our perspective is clear, we realize that God is really the one making the sacrifices. He alone pays the price of the costly gift of grace. And what he starts in our lives, he finishes. It is an inexorable law. He refuses to leave us as we are.

I warned the reader in the very first sentence of the preface that this is a scandalous book because of its subject-matter. Jesus' parable of the landowner (Matt. 20:1–16) brings out the scandal of grace perhaps better than any other story that he told. It is interesting that Matthew—the tax collector—is the only gospel writer to include this story. Perhaps because it dealt with economic issues, it was especially poignant for Matthew. But that is exactly the rub: It was seemingly so unfair eco-

---
[23] Blomberg, *Interpreting the Parables*, 279.

nomically for the landowner in the story to pay the same wage to those who were hired at five o'clock as those who had worked all or most of the day. If American businesses operated on this principle there would be economic chaos—and massive riots!

Philip Yancey writes that we need to learn "the new math of grace" before we will ever get the point of this and similar stories in the gospels.[24] This parable teaches us that grace is never earned. Whether we have lived the life of faith all our lives, or we have a deathbed conversion, the result is the same: We all get to enjoy together the bliss of heaven! The grumblers in the story correspond to Jesus' religious opponents in his day, as well as, unfortunately, to many "Christians" today who have simply never "got it." God loves *everyone*—liberals, conservatives, Democrats, Republicans, unethical business executives, pimps, prostitutes, perverts, mobsters, con-men, terrorists, … and even Baptists, Presbyterians, charismatics, Catholics, and the like. Jesus went after the least "deserving"—he still does. If we don't understand this, we simply don't understand grace (or the doctrine of original sin, for that matter). America, it's either greed or grace. Which will it be? I, for one, choose the new math of grace. But we would be remiss to conclude this section on Jesus' parables without looking at three parables of grace Luke collected for us.

The lost sheep (Luke 15:3–7; Matt. 18:10–14), the lost coin (Luke 15:8–10), and the lost son (Luke 15:11–32) are parables of grace par excellence. They teach a loving God who simply cherishes lost people and is ecstatic when they are found. ("Lost" is one of those unique words that means roughly the same in both secular and religious parlance.) The third parable of the three, the most developed one, is the best known. It is unforgettable. Any loving parent cannot help but be moved by the waiting father in this story. As Jeremias writes: "The parable describes with touching simplicity what God is like, his goodness, his grace, his boundless mercy, his abounding love."[25] It also zeroes in on both religious and secular pride. Donald Guthrie makes this apt observation:

---
[24] Yancey, *What's So Amazing About Grace?*, 59–72.
[25] Jeremias, *The Parables of Jesus*, 131.

The parable was an answer to the murmuring of the Pharisees, who found it inconceivable that God would bestow grace apart from any merit on man's part. The merit-conscious elder son was in fact incapable of even recognizing his father's grace towards his brother.[26]

And so it is today. We are scandalized and skeptical when a known scoundrel claims to have experienced divine grace. Let them get what they deserve. If the enemy of our souls cannot keep us trapped in worldliness, he is just as content to trip us up with spiritual pride. And the latter, believe it or not, is even more deadly and destructive. More churches have been ruined and more people kept out of the kingdom by the spiritual pride of supposedly the most pious saints than by any other sin. It's sort of like the charismatic who at first is inhibited about raising his hands in worship because of personal pride but who later looks down his superior nose at those who still shy away from this gesture.

The General Epistles

Before we turn to *the* theologian of grace in the New Testament, the apostle Paul, we must look briefly into the general epistles. The letter to the Hebrews demonstrates the unity of the Scriptures concerning God's gracious plan of redemption. It all leads up to Jesus, who brings a new and better covenant. "That salvation is of grace is seen from the statement in Hebrews 2:9 about Jesus that 'by the grace of God he might taste death for every one.'"[27] It is through Christ's substitutionary atoning death alone that we are saved. Further, Hebrews exhorts us: "Let us therefore approach the throne of grace with boldness, so that we may receive mercy and find grace to help in time of need" (Heb. 4:16). We must first note that it is a *throne* that we are approaching. "The heavenly throne is a symbol of the sovereignty of God."[28] But through Christ as our high priest (Heb. 4:14–16) we can approach

---
[26] Guthrie, *New Testament Theology*, 605–06.
[27] Guthrie, *New Testament Theology*, 629.
[28] Gurhrie, *New Testament Theology*, 882.

with boldness, receive mercy, and find grace—because it is a throne of *grace*! The great prince of preachers, Charles Spurgeon, could wax eloquent on this glorious truth.

In relation to prayer, Spurgeon exhorts us to ask "for great things, for you are before a great throne." Grace conquers sin and is all-powerful. "The mercy seat is a throne." "On the throne of grace, sovereignty has placed itself under the bonds of love." Spurgeon would remind us as well of the cost of saving grace in Jesus' blood and would encourage us boldly to claim God's promises in our lives of prayer and faith.[29]

Continuing our journey through the general epistles, we find that even the letter of James, which Luther called "one strawy epistle," sounds the note of grace. In the midst of his discussion of disputes among the saints and of worldliness (James 4:1-5), James announces good news: "But he gives all the more grace" (v. 6). The Christian life not only begins in grace but also continues in grace—grace for every situation. Thus, James follows this encouragement with an exhortation to humility (quoting Prov. 3:34), to submitting to God, resisting the devil, drawing near to God, cleansing from sin, purifying the heart, repentance, and mourning (vv. 6-10). God's grace at work in our lives brings about these results, and we are expected to cooperate with this grace. In other words, instead of the passivity we too often see in relation to sanctification and spiritual maturity in our day, we are, as the Puritans did, to *actively pursue* this holiness and godliness. "Humble yourselves before the Lord," James says, "and he will exalt you." We do the humbling, and God does the exalting.

Finally, the apostle Peter adds his voice. He describes our relationships in the church in terms of a charismatic community: We are to be "good stewards of the manifold grace [*charis*] of God" because each of us has received a gift (*charisma*), whether in speaking or in serving (1 Peter 4:10-11). Grace is variegated like the rainbow. It

---

[29] Charles Spurgeon, "The Throne of Grace" in *The Power of Prayer in the Believer's Life*, compiled and edited by Robert Hall (Lynwood, Washington: Emerald Books, 1993), 15-28 (part of series of volumes: Charles Spurgeon Christian Living Classics).

marks each of us for a place of service in the church for the ultimate purpose that "God may be glorified in all things through Jesus Christ" (v. 11). As we saw in our survey of the gospel of John, Peter knew well, by personal experience, the grace of God. That is why the first half of Luke's Acts narrative (chapters 1–12) could well be entitled "The Acts of Peter." It is to the central figure in the second half of Acts (chapters 13–28)—in what might be called "The Acts of Paul"—that we now turn.

Paul

The apostle Paul, whose life, like Peter's, was dramatically transformed by God's grace, might be called the "systematic theologian of grace." It is no surprise that in our discussions—and debates!—surrounding grace that Paul is the New Testament writer to whom we most often refer. "Paul was the first and greatest Christian theologian."[30] And perhaps no New Testament theologian has better penetrated into the heart of both Paul's theology and his religious experience than James D. G. Dunn. I will be citing Dunn's conclusions at length in this presentation of Paul. It might be argued that the apostle Paul single handedly set out grace as *the* Christian theological distinctive:

> Among the most innovative features which shaped Christian theology for all time are the key terms which Paul introduced. Above all we should think of "gospel," "grace," and "love"—gospel as the good news of Christ focusing in his death and resurrection, grace as epitomizing the character of God's dealings with humankind, love as the motive of divine giving and in turn the motive for human living. Between them, in their specialist Christian usage, these words sum up and define the scope and character of Christianity as no other three words can. And that specialist Christian usage, in each case, we owe entirely to Paul.[31]

---

[30] James D. G. Dunn, *The Theology of Paul the Apostle* (Grand Rapids, Mich.: Eerdmans, 1998), 2.
[31] Dunn, *The Theology of Paul the Apostle*, 733.

Gospel, grace, and love: These realities are inseparable. And to explore grace, which is the focus of this brief study, is to mine the riches of the gospel and of the love of God.

Grace is more caught than taught. That is why it is often easier to grasp grace by observing Jesus in action, having meals with social and religious outcasts,—"sinners," as they were often called—honoring women and children, who were treated like chattel in his day, touching and healing lepers, and, supremely, going to the cross. Also, as we have already seen, contemplating Jesus' parables provides access and insight into grace. All these avenues were meant to enable us to *experience* grace. Experience often precedes understanding. This was certainly true in Paul's case. A zealous Pharisee bent on persecuting purveyors of the gospel of grace, Paul had to be arrested on the road to Damascus by the Lord himself and experience this grace firsthand before he could fully begin to understand it. Perception preceded conception.

> For Paul, grace is God's transforming power in action on our behalf. It is God's Spirit invading our lives and changing us.

Again, Dunn provides an apt summary:

> It was [Paul's] own *experience of grace* which made "grace" a central and distinctive feature of his gospel—grace as not merely a way of understanding God as generous and forgiving, but grace as the experience of that unmerited and free acceptance embracing him, transforming him, enriching him, commissioning him (e.g., Rom. 5:2, 17; 12:6; 1 Cor. 1:4–5; 15:10; 2 Cor. 9:14; 12:9; Gal. 2:9; Eph. 1:7–8; 3:7–8).[32]

For Paul, grace is God's transforming power *in action* on our behalf. It is God's Spirit invading our lives and changing us. There is such a close

---

[32] James D. G. Dunn, *Unity and Diversity in the New Testament: An Inquiry into the Character of Earliest Christianity* (Philadelphia: Westminster, 1977), 190.

relation between Paul's understanding of the Spirit and his concept of grace that in any given Pauline passage one could substitute one term for the other without substantially altering the significance of the passage![33]

Paul's gospel then was an extrapolation of this dynamic experience of grace. He had accepted God's free gift of righteousness and felt compelled by this same grace to herald the good news to the world! Dunn provides this summary of Paul's understanding of the gospel:

> For Paul the essence of Christianity is acceptance by God (justification) in an intimate relationship, entered into and lived in by faith on man's side, made possible and empowered by the gift of grace, the gift of the Spirit (see particularly Rom 3:21–5:21; Gal. 2:16–4:7). This seems to be the core of Paul's kerygma, distinctive both in its central emphases and in its developed expression.[34]

Paul's own programmatic statement at the beginning of "The Gospel According to Paul," Romans, reads as follows:

> I am not ashamed of the gospel, because it is the power of God that brings salvation to everyone who believes: first to the Jew, then to the Gentile. For in the gospel the righteousness of God is revealed—a righteousness that is by faith from first to last, just as it is written: "The righteous will live by faith" (Rom. 1:16–17 TNIV).

"For Paul, the revelation of the righteousness of God *is* the gospel."[35] One becomes immediately aware that Paul set the parameters for how the church would conceptualize the doctrine of grace for the next two millennia! However, Paul's utilization of the term *grace* is significantly more nuanced than has generally been acknowledged. Again, Dunn is a sure guide into these complexities.

First, grace in Paul's writings can be used to refer to *the historical event of Jesus Christ*. "For you know the grace of our Lord Jesus Christ,

---

[33] Compare James D. G. Dunn, *Jesus and the Spirit: A Study of the Religious and Charismatic Experience of Jesus and the First Christians as Reflected in the New Testament* (London: SCM Press, 1975), 204.
[34] Dunn, *Unity and Diversity in the New Testament*, 22–23.
[35] Alister E. McGrath, *Iustitia Dei: A History of the Christian Doctrine of Justification*, 2nd ed. (Cambridge: UK: Cambridge University Press, 1998), 4. This study by McGrath stands without parallel as a definitive history of the doctrine of justification and, therefore, of the doctrine of grace.

that though he was rich, yet for your sake he became poor, so that you through his poverty might become rich" (2 Cor. 8:9 TNIV). Grace is God's becoming a human being as the Word made flesh, to use John's language. Christ takes on our poverty in exchange for his riches. The Christ-event, in which God walked across the pages of history and went to the cross for our redemption, is grace in action. In his Roman epistle, Paul refers to "God's grace and the gift that came by the grace of the one man, Jesus Christ" (Rom. 5:15 TNIV). For Paul, the Christ-event makes a law-based righteousness obsolete: "I do not nullify the grace of God; for if justification comes through the law, then Christ died for nothing" (Gal. 2:21). The doxology which begins the Ephesian epistle contains these words pointing to this same reality: "to the praise of his glorious grace that he freely bestowed on us in the Beloved. In him we have redemption through his blood, the forgiveness of our trespasses, according to the riches of his grace that he lavished on us" (Eph. 1:6–7).[36] Christmas and Easter, then, commemorate grace as the historical event of Jesus.

This same Ephesian epistle makes reference to another dimension of grace as presented by Paul: *the grace of conversion* (see Rom. 3:24; 5:15, 17, 20; 1 Cor. 1:4–5; 15:10; 2 Cor. 6:1; Gal. 1:6; 2:21; Eph. 2:5, 8). One of the best known passages in Ephesians reads as follows: "For by grace you have been saved through faith, and this is not your own doing; it is the gift of God—not the result of works, so that no one may boast" (Eph.2:8–9). Our salvation is all God's doing, including the personal beginning point of conversion. Paul repeats this principle twice in this chapter: "by grace you have been saved" (vv. 5, 8). He then goes on to indicate, "For we are God's masterpiece. He has created us anew in Christ Jesus, so that we can do the good things he planned for us long ago (v. 10 NLT). Thus, our entire lives are God's workmanship; it is grace from start to finish in the Christian pilgrimage.[37]

Grace is also for Paul, therefore, *the present transforming presence and power of God*. It is a "grace in which we stand" (Rom. 5:2). Grace

---

[36] Dunn, *Jesus and the Spirit*, 202.
[37] Dunn, *Jesus and the Spirit*, 202.

empowers us to overcome sin and live godly lives (Rom. 5:21; 6:14; 2 Cor. 1:12). Paul was able to endure and even rejoice in suffering because the Lord had told him, "My grace is sufficient for you, for my power is made perfect in weakness" (2 Cor. 12:9 TNIV, ESV). Notice the parallel between grace and power. To go back under the law, seeking justification by religious performance, is to be cut off from Christ and to fall away from grace (Gal. 5:4). It is by grace alone that we are converted and that we make progress in our Christian lives. How easily we can fall back into a "performance syndrome" in our walk with Christ! Thus, the best thing Paul could wish his converts (see the greetings in his letters) was God's grace—"the gracious power of God existentially moving in and upon their lives."[38]

Further, there was in Paul an awareness of a *commissioning grace* that called forth his apostleship and calls each Christian to a place of service as well: "For by the grace given to me I say to everyone among you not to think of yourself more highly than you ought to think.... We have gifts that differ according to the grace given to us" (Rom. 12:3, 6). In this same letter, Paul makes reference to "the grace given me by God to be a minister of Christ Jesus to the Gentiles in the priestly service of the gospel of God" (Rom. 15:15–16; see also Rom. 1:5; 1 Cor. 3:10; Gal. 2:9; Eph. 3:2, 7–8). In other words, Paul felt that all believers "should have some sort of *awareness* of the particular manifestation of grace in their lives."[39] But do we? One of the weaknesses of the contemporary church is that we too often do not have such an awareness of God's commissioning grace. Our churches are significantly weakened thereby.

Finally, Paul uses the term *grace* to refer to the church's (or the apostle's—see, for example, 2 Cor. 1:15) *actual ministry* itself. He consistently refers to the collection he was gathering for the needy saints of Jerusalem as a "grace" (1 Cor. 16:3; 2 Cor. 8:1, 4, 6–7, 19). Thus, we see many dimensions to grace in Paul. Grace is a dynamic power, in Paul's understanding. It is God *in action* on our behalf. Grace is also personal

---
[38] Dunn, *Jesus and the Spirit*, 203.
[39] Dunn, *Jesus and the Spirit*, 203.

in terms of our own experience of salvation, sanctification, and service. And grace is *total* in scope. "*The whole of life is for Paul an expression of grace: all is of grace and grace is all.*"⁴⁰ In addition, Dunn argues that our failure to appreciate the *experiential* nature of grace in Paul has too often resulted in our distorting his other teachings.

Dunn's comments concerning this reality have far-reaching implications for current debates on grace:

> Perhaps the classic example of the failure to appreciate the extent to which Paul's theology is the expression of his experience is the *doctrine* of predestination. So far as Paul is concerned the idea of election speaks neither of an immutable law of God nor of an implacable law of nature, but is simply, in Otto's words, "an immediate and pure expression of the actual religious experience of grace."⁴¹

Much more will be said about this later. But one wonders whether we have too often attempted to penetrate the mysterious workings of God in speculative fashion and thereby lost the wonder of it all. Calvinist or Arminian, our first response to grace should be doxological! Amazing grace ... that saved a wretch like me. We may also read too much into some of Paul's statements in our speculations concerning the eternal counsels of God. Maintaining sanity and balance in such debates is totally the work of God's grace!

In his *Theology of Paul the Apostle,* Dunn provides a handy one-paragraph summary of the above presentation and adds further helpful comments.⁴² First, Dunn notes Paul's unique usage of *charis* in relation to the Septuagint's usage of *chen* and *chesed.* Paul apparently joined the positive aspects of each of the Hebrew terms in his use of *charis,* combining the "unilateralness of *chen* and the lasting commitment of *chesed.*"⁴³ Thus, grace is seen to be totally from God's side and also ex-

---

⁴⁰ Dunn, *Jesus and the Spirit,* 203–05 (quotation from 204–05). Dunn's summary comments in this section are quite illuminating and edifying.

⁴¹ Dunn, *Jesus and the Spirit,* 200. Dunn cites Rudolf Otto, *The Idea of the Holy* (Oxford, UK: Oxford University Press, 1923), 91.

⁴² Dunn, *The Theology of Paul the Apostle,* 319–20.

⁴³ Dunn, *The Theology of Paul the Apostle,* 321.

presses his covenant faithfulness. One common usage of grace in Paul's day was in reference to benefactions or acts of charity. Viewing such inscriptions would have been a daily occurrence. Again, the background for God's benefaction of salvation to humanity is obvious. Thus, grace is a gift. Grace is power. And grace proliferates: "Grace begets grace." Grace points to the gift or ministry itself, the gratitude for such, and the community that is created by these loving actions.[44] It truly is an all-encompassing concept in Paul's theology.

All of these ideas relate, in the main, to the Christian community. Our goal has been, thus far, to grasp the overall concept of grace in the Bible. But there is a broader idea of grace which applies to all people, at all times, and in all places. Theologians often refer to this concept as common grace or providence. Jesus taught about this grace. The Scriptures in general teach this doctrine. And it is to this very edifying topic that we must now turn our attention.

---

[44] Dunn, *The Theology of Paul the Apostle*, 319–23.

Chapter Five:
Common Grace

IN PERHAPS THE BEST KNOWN VERSE IN THE BIBLE we read: "For God loved the world so much that he gave his only Son, so that everyone who believes in him may not die but have eternal life" (John 3:16 GNT). What makes this verse even more astounding is the "world" referred to here that God loves so much. John uses the term *kosmos*, which generally in John's gospel refers to the evil world system set against God and his kingdom. It is this sinful, rebellious world that God loves so much. In the Sermon on the Mount, Jesus refers to God's universal benevolence in another way: "He gives his best—the sun to warm and the rain to nourish—to everyone, regardless: the good and the bad, the nice and the nasty" (Matt. 5:45 The Message). "The Most High," Luke quotes Jesus as saying, "is kind to the ungrateful and the wicked"; he is a "merciful" Father (Luke 6:35–36). So God loves everybody, good or bad. Clearly, this is grace. In this chapter we want to study this grace that every person experiences every day of their life—Christian, Muslim, Buddhist, atheist, whoever.

The two broad categories for the doctrine of grace are *common grace* and *special grace*. In this chapter we will examine common grace and in the next chapter special grace. This division is similar to the two broad categories of the doctrine of revelation: general revelation and special revelation. General revelation, like common grace, applies to all people, at all times, and in all places. Special revelation, like special grace, is a *saving* revelation. In the doctrine of creation, consideration is generally given to divine providence. The doctrine of providence and common grace refer to roughly the same reality. More precisely, one may correlate general providence (God's working in and through the natural order) with common grace and special providence (God's redemptive intervention) with special grace. As is true with these and other related doctrines, the varied forms of grace must be seen both in terms of their *distinction* and their *relation*. First, some definitions are in order.

Definitions

Thomas Oden defines common grace as follows: "That grace is called *common* which is shared by all humanity even amid all conceivable forms of fallenness. The gifts offered by God are never common in the sense of ordinary, profane, and petty, but in the sense of being universally offered to all."[1] Thus, by common grace we mean a universal grace, but not a universalism. Just as general revelation in creation and conscience is not a saving revelation but rather holds us accountable to God (Rom. 1, 2), so common grace brings countless blessings into every person's life, but does not bring eternal redemption.[2] Common grace, as defined by Millard Erickson, is a grace "extended to all persons through God's general providence."[3] Common grace restrains sin and evil, thus preserving human civilization, and brings innumerable blessings—the beauty of nature and its bountiful fruits, food, friendship, design, and purpose (the list is endless) to every person.[4] "Common grace is the undeserved beneficence of the Creator God expressed by his general care of creation and of all persons everywhere without discrimination" (Pss. 36:5; 119:64; 136:1–9).[5] Secular opponents of the faith argue that the problem of evil flies in the face of this doctrine. But is this really so?

The Problem of Good

My experience in witnessing to intellectuals is that they invariably bring up the conundrum of evil as a challenge to the faith being recom-

---
[1] Thomas C. Oden, *The Transforming Power of Grace* (Nashville: Abingdon, 1993), 63.
[2] See Wayne Grudem, *Systematic Theology* (Grand Rapids, Mich.: Zondervan, 1994), 657.
[3] Millard J. Erickson, *Concise Dictionary of Christian Theology* (Grand Rapids, Mich.: Baker, 1986), 69.
[4] See M. Eugene Osterhaven, "Common Grace" in *Basic Christian Doctrine*, ed. Carl F. H. Henry (Grand Rapids, Mich.: Baker, 1962), 69.
[5] Bruce Demarest, *The Cross and Salvation* (Wheaton, Ill.: Crossway Books, 1997), 76.

mended to them. I have learned to counter this supposed obstacle with the "problem of good." Why is there so much good in the world? This is the message of common grace. In view of our fallenness, we should be asking, Why do good things happen to bad people? not the obverse![6] Once Jesus was told about some Galilean Jews who were killed in the temple by Pilate *while they were offering their sacrifices!* Jesus added the tragic story about the eighteen people upon whom the Tower of Siloam, perhaps near the Pool of Siloam in southeast Jerusalem, fell. Were all these people worse sinners than others? Jesus answered with an emphatic no, and added, "unless you repent, you will all perish just as they did" (Luke 13:1–5). Grace and judgment again come together—judgment facing us all, *because we deserve it*, and the gracious offer of repentance and forgiveness.

> Why is there so much good in the world? This is the message of common grace.

I am amazed at how easily we want to make evil God's problem. So, to solve his problem for him we will argue, as Rabbi Harold Kushner did, that God is simply not omnipotent and, therefore, couldn't prevent the particular tragedy that troubles us. More recently, open theists have tried a similar ploy, attributing the problem to an open future that even God doesn't know. God has limits like us and empathizes with us in our misery. But how comforting is such a belief, really? Not very much! This is not to treat human misery in a cavalier fashion. The questions are there, and there are no foolproof answers for us this side of heaven. All I am saying is that the reality of common grace balances out the picture for us. We too often have tunnel vision in such discussions.

The greater problem of good confronts us with our own personal evil. As Isaiah wrote (Isa. 26:10):

> Though grace is shown to the wicked,
> they do not learn righteousness;

---
[6] This insight and the discussion to follow are based on James Boice's excellent sermon on common grace found in: James Montgomery Boice, *Amazing Grace* (Wheaton, Ill.: Tyndale House, 1993), 17–28.

> even in a land of uprightness they go on doing evil
> and regard not the majesty of the Lord.

Therefore, in our sinful pride, we avert our eyes from all the good which inundates our lives and harangue God or his people about all the evil in the world.

In the face of the paganism of his own day, Paul preached this common grace:

> In past generations he allowed all nations to follow their own ways; yet he has not left himself without a witness in doing good—giving you rains from heaven and fruitful seasons, and filling you with food and your hearts with joy (Acts 14:16–17).

We see in these words four expressions of common grace: (1) delay of judgment, (2) rain, (3) crops and food, and (4) joy. At Athens Paul preached the same thing: "He gives life, breath, and everything else to all people" (Acts 17:25 CEV). And further: "From one person God made all nations who live on earth, and he decided when and where every nation would be" (v. 26 CEV). Common grace encompasses, therefore, all our personal and national lives. It accounts for all nobler aspects of the diverse cultures on this planet. As Francis Schaeffer was always quick to remind us, the image of God in humanity was not *annihilated* at the fall. Therefore, Christians, above all others, should be able to appreciate and celebrate the beauty and significance of every worthy cultural expression. Consequently, we should not lose sight of common grace and the "problem of good" as we reflect on the meaning of our lives in this fallen world.

Dimensions of Common Grace

> The Lord is gracious and merciful,
>   slow to anger and abounding in steadfast love.
> The Lord is good to all,
>   And his compassion is over all that he has made.

With these majestic words (Ps. 145:8–9), David celebrates the goodness of God in common grace. James would add: "Every generous act of giving, with every perfect gift, is from above, coming down from the Father of lights, with whom there is no variation or shadow due to change" (James 1:17). But what are the dimensions of this grace? Wayne Grudem delineates at least six.[7]

David, for example, in the psalm just mentioned, refers to common grace in the *physical realm* with these words: "The eyes of all look to you, and you give them their food in due season. You open your hand, satisfying the desire of every living creature" (Ps. 145:15–16). "The earth is the LORD's," David says in another well known psalm, "and all that is in it, the world, and those who live in it" (Ps. 24:1). The biblical portrait of our Creator is of a God who is intimately involved with every aspect of his creation. He feeds the birds and clothes the grass of the field, so should we ever be anxious about such matters (Matt. 6:25–34)? The biblical teaching on common grace reminds us that God is interested in our *physical* needs.

Common grace extends to the *intellectual realm* as well. John's prologue contains these intriguing words: "The true light, which enlightens everyone, was coming into the world" (John 1:9). Any true "enlightenment" intellectually has its source in Christ, according to John. This common grace (and general revelation) provides the point of contact for Christian apologetics and evangelism. But, as we shall see, it takes the gracious work of the Holy Spirit in special grace to bring someone to a saving knowledge of the Lord. John Calvin wrote:

> Some men excel in keenness; others are superior in judgment; still others have a readier wit to learn this or that art. In this variety God commends his grace to us, lest anyone should claim as his own what flowed from the sheer bounty of God.[8]

---

[7] Grudem, *Systematic Theology*, 658–62. I have adopted and adapted Grudem's helpful delineation of realms of common grace in the presentation that follows.

[8] John Calvin, *Institutes of the Christian Religion*, 2 vols., ed. John T. McNeill, trans. Ford Lewis Battles (Philadelphia: Westminster, 1960), 276 (II.ii.7).

Thus, any blessings which we enjoy from science and technology (such as this computer on which I am typing) we owe to common grace, to our good and generous God. In fact, as Calvin was saying, any praise for excellence in any of the arts or sciences is ultimately owed to God.

The *moral realm* is another dimension of common grace. The general revelation of God in the human conscience (Rom. 2:14–16) provides a moral compass for humankind. Unfortunately, this innate moral understanding has been distorted by sin. Nonetheless, even the most pagan of cultures has some sort of code of right and wrong. Jesus said that even sinners "do good" to those who do good to them (Luke 6:33). The problem with both Jew and Gentile, however, is that they "suppress the truth" about God and his righteousness and oppose his kingdom (Rom. 1:18–23). All of us, therefore, remain "without excuse" (v. 20) before Holy God.

Since there remains a vestigial remnant of the *imago dei* in humankind, we still evince tremendous imaginative and inventive abilities. This reality reflects the *creative realm* of common grace. In actuality, Calvin made reference to this dimension in the previous quote. There is a dignity, beauty, and creativity to humanity that should astound us and prompt us to glorify God. Too often Christians have been remiss in this regard. We are sometimes hesitant, for example, to acknowledge the dignity, brilliance, and creativity of the unbeliever, which consequently damages our witness and influence. Especially is this true in terms of our relation to the creative arts. A full appreciation for common grace should move us a little more toward the "Christ transforming culture" (Niebuhr) orientation and toward being more of a leavening influence in the arts. Popular culture seems so shallow and perverse so often that we naturally tend toward retreat. But belief in common grace won't allow us that luxury.[9]

Common grace also superintends in the *societal realm*. According to Paul, for example, God himself ordained the functions of the state

---

[9] See, for example, William D. Romanowski's *Eyes Wide Open: Looking for God in Popular Culture* (Grand Rapid, Mich.: Brazos Press, 2001).

(Rom. 13:1–9). In his providential care God curbs evil so that we are rarely as bad as we could possibly be. That hell will lack this common grace is in part what constitutes hell as hell. Other structures of society can also reflect the influence of common grace. The family, of course, was God's first societal institution. One can certainly see the influence of Christianity upon educational and eleemosynary institutions. The list is almost endless. Common grace can be operative through all of these for the benefit of humanity. Sin and evil, of course, may also distort and utilize these same structures.

Finally, even in the *religious realm* common grace is at work. Did not Paul bear at least indirect witness to this truth in his Mars Hill address (Acts 17:22–31)? Some pluralists have attempted to transform this common grace into special, saving grace, but Scripture does not warrant this move. Distortion, destruction, and even the demonic can be found in the religious realm as well. Nevertheless, humanity's incurably religious nature continually seeks after ultimate realities. Philosophers in our day may have largely given up on metaphysics, but the average person continues to ask these questions. Paul appealed to this religious reality that day in Athens.

What has become apparent in these explorations is that the doctrine of providence must be included in any full-orbed understanding of common grace. Rooted as it is in the doctrine of creation, the doctrine of providence has generally been given more attention than the doctrine of common grace. The two doctrines are integral, if not identical, however. Common grace, if mentioned at all, generally comes up for consideration in soteriology, being contrasted with special grace. If for no other reason that clarifying God's benevolence toward humanity, any discussion of common grace should include comments on providence as well. How does God relate to his creation? What kind of benevolence and care can we expect from God as humans? As believers? How does God's care and control of things relate to our prayers? In the final two sections of this chapter, we want to consider such matters.

Providence

John Calvin penned one of the best statements on the meaning and importance of providence that I have ever read:

> Moreover to make God a momentary Creator, who once for all finished his work, would be cold and barren, and we must differ from profane men specially in that we see the presence of divine power shining as much in the continuing state of the universe as in its inception. For even though the minds of the impious too are compelled by merely looking upon earth and heaven to rise up to the Creator, yet faith has its own peculiar way of assigning the whole credit for Creation to God. To this pertains that saying of the apostle's, to which we have referred before, that only "by faith we understand that the universe was created by the word of God" [Heb. 11:3]. For unless we pass on to his providence—however we may seem both to comprehend with the mind and to confess with the tongue—we do not yet properly grasp what it means to say: "God is Creator." Carnal sense, once confronted with the power of God in the very Creation, stops there, and at most weighs and contemplates only the wisdom, power, and goodness of the author in accomplishing such handiwork. (These matters are self-evident, and even force themselves upon the unwilling.) It contemplates, moreover, some general preserving and governing activity, from which the force of motion derives. In short, carnal sense thinks there is an energy divinely bestowed from the beginning, sufficient to sustain all things.
>
> But faith ought to penetrate more deeply, namely, having found him Creator of all, forthwith to conclude he is also everlasting Governor and Preserver—not only in that he drives the celestial frame as well as its several parts by a universal motion, but also in that he sustains, nourishes, and cares for, everything he has made, even to the least sparrow [cf. Matt. 10:29].[10]

God is not a "momentary Creator," Calvin teaches us. Rather, God "sustains, nourishes, and cares" for his creation. God is "everlasting Governor and Preserver" of the universe. Providence means, literally, that God sees ahead and provides. He manages, oversees, and rules. He

---
[10] Calvin, *Institutes*, 197–98 (I.xvi.1).

orders everything, yet allows his creatures real (though limited) freedom. God need not be a "micromanager" to have everything under control. He is wiser and more powerful than that!

Predictably, a number of competing ways of conceptualizing this reality have emerged, ranging from deism to fatalism.[11] Among theologians, deistic (some neo-liberals), dynamic (process and openness views), dominion (church dominion model), and directive (redemptive intervention model) orientations are evident, alongside views indebted to the thinking of Luis de Molina, Thomas Aquinas, Karl Barth, or John Calvin. Presenting and evaluating such views would range far beyond the purview of this modest volume. What will be presented here is an eclectic model, which will hopefully be able to draw insights from many of the above perspectives.

Conceptualizing providence inevitably entails integrating biblical, theological, and philosophical insights. One's views of God, freedom, time, and eternity determine definitively one's doctrine of providence. For example, if God truly "sees ahead," as providence has traditionally been conceived, then can a process or openness model of providence really work? On the other hand, if God truly controls everything, then can humanity honestly be characterized as having authentic freedom? These are hot issues at present among evangelicals.[12] What follows is *one* way of approaching these knotty questions. There are other viable options.

First, we must examine our doctrine of God. I am assuming traditional categories here. God is *omniscient*. He is all-knowing. He knows exhaustively the past, present, and future. He has *natural knowledge* of the causal process, *middle knowledge* of all possible worlds and all that *could* happen given specific parameters (which he sets), and *free knowledge* of all that *does* happen. The informed and alert reader will note

---

[11] Terrence Tiessen has provided perhaps the best survey of options to date: *Providence and Prayer* (Downers Grove, Ill.: InterVarsity Press, 2000).
[12] In my view, the best analysis of the biblical, theological, philosophical, and practical issues in this debate (primarily with open theism) at the time of this writing is Millard J. Erickson's *What Does God Know and When Does He Know It?* (Grand Rapids, Mich.: Zondervan, 2003).

that I am using the categories of Molinism here and that the nature of God's knowledge is precisely what is being debated in evangelicalism at present. However, I am not limiting myself solely to the insights of this particular model and do not pretend to have the final word on this debate.

Second, God is *omnipotent*. He is all-powerful. He can do anything that is consistent with his character. He is also *free*: "Our God is in the heavens; he does whatever he pleases" (Ps. 115:3). He can accomplish his sovereign purposes with or without our cooperation. He can loosen or tighten his control according to his holy and loving desires and purposes.

Third, God is *omnipresent*, everywhere present to the created order. At this juncture, it is helpful to introduce the fundamental theological concepts of immanence and transcendence. In my own systematic theology, I elaborate on God's essence as spirit in terms of immanence and transcendence.[13] Immanence refers to God's omnipresence. Transcendence refers to God's being "wholly other" than, "outside" of, and independent from the created order. In our day, there has been a massive loss of transcendence in the prevailing understandings of God. God's words through Isaiah need to be heard again:

> For thus says the high and lofty one
> who inhabits eternity, whose name is Holy:
> I dwell in the high and holy place,
> and also with those who are contrite and humble in spirit,
> to revive the spirit of the humble,
> and to revive the heart of the contrite (Isa. 57:15).

God in his transcendent holiness inhabits eternity, but he also offers a special immanence with the humble and contrite. Immanence and transcendence must always be held in balance, in order to be faithful to the biblical portrait of God. These concepts seem especially relevant to current debates concerning providence.

The question is raised whether our actions and decisions can truly be free if God already knows what they are going to be. The answer is

---

[13] Larry D. Hart, *Truth Aflame* (Grand Rapids, Mich.: Zondervan, 2005), 78–80.

yes to both propositions. I know my wife's personality intimately and can often predict her future words and actions. How much more so the God of infinite knowledge of all things! Then how does one deal with those biblical passages in which God seemingly shows grief and disappointment with his chosen people and their decisions? The answer lies with God's immanence and transcendence. God is immanent and transcendent to *both* space and time. Thus, in his transcendence he can foreknow the future exhaustively, while in his immanence he can interact with his creatures in both space and time. The Incarnation itself demonstrates this principle.[14]

It seems to me that maintaining this balance is the key to current debates.[15] Most do not quibble with God's immanence and transcendence with relation to *space*. They can easily accept both God's existence outside of the universe and his intimate relation to it. What is most often overlooked, however, is that space and time are intertwined and inseparable. God is *also*, therefore, *both* outside of and independent of time, while at the same time intimately related to the ongoing flow of the events of time. We have, therefore, inadvertently put limits upon God when we argue that his foreknowing our future decisions means his predetermining those decisions. That is the fallacy we see on both extremes—open theism and extreme Calvinism. Holding to "free will," open theism denies divine foreknowledge of future free decisions. Holding to divine foreknowledge, extreme Calvinism is perceived by many to be denying free choice. Both positions are in error because of the shared false premise. Divine foreknowledge simply does not preclude (finite) human freedom. Augustine saw this clearly:

> The conclusion is that we are by no means under compulsion to abandon free choice in favor of divine foreknowledge, nor need

---
[14] Compare Millard J. Erickson, *God the Father Almighty* (Grand Rapids, Mich.: Baker, 1998), 274–77.
[15] Stanley J. Grenz and Roger E. Olson have demonstrated that this immanence/transcendence issue is key to evaluating all theological systems: *Twentieth-Century Theology* (Downers Grove, Ill.: InterVarsity Press, 1992).

we deny—God forbid!—that God knows the future, as a condition for holding free choice.[16]

Clearly both of these contemporary extremes need to heed Augustine's counsel. Therefore, it is important to note that *moderate* forms of both Calvinism and Arminianism will affirm both propositions: divine sovereignty and human freedom (or responsibility).

The doctrines of providence and common grace teach that God has everything under control and is working out his good purposes for his creation. Does this mean that God's will is always done? This is a dangerous question to answer. A simple yes or no might be misleading. In one sense, the Bible is crystal clear that God's will *is* always done. Everything happens either by God's action or God's permission. This is what is meant by the sovereignty of God. Everything happens "according to the plan of him who works out everything in conformity with the purpose of his will" (Eph. 1:11 TNIV).[17] At the same time, Jesus himself taught us to pray, "Your kingdom come. Your will be done, on earth as it is in heaven" (Matt. 6:10). If God's will, in this sense, were perfectly done there would be heaven on earth. Where God rules supremely there is no sin, sickness, sorrow, or death. Obviously, Jesus is teaching us to pray for something that has not yet been completely actualized. The kingdom was inaugurated at Jesus' first coming, but it will only be consummated at his second coming. So in this second sense God's will is not always done.

> The doctrines of providence and common grace teach that God has everything under control and is working out his good purposes for his creation.

---

[16] Augustine, *City of God* (5.10) cited in Norman Geisler, *Chosen But Free* (Minneapolis, Minn.: Bethany House, 1999), 165.

[17] In this particular verse Paul is referring to our being elected and predestined in Christ, which we will consider in the next chapter on special grace. The principle of divine sovereignty expressed here, however, is universally applicable.

There are a number of false alternatives to providence:

> *Indeterminism* says that God is not in control and, therefore, his will is not done. *Determinism* says that God's control is so absolute that in effect human freedom and responsibility are canceled. *Omnicausality* says that God does everything and his creation does nothing. *Chance* says that no personal or rational power is in control. And *fate* says that the ultimate power is not necessarily benevolent.[18]

But what does the Bible say? Jack Cottrell has provided a comprehensive response to this question from an Arminian perspective.[19] I have adapted "Cottrell's categories," as I call them, to teach on the subject of God's will both in the seminary classroom and in the local church setting. The response has always been encouraging.

God's will, in terms of his providential control, can generally be summarized under three rubrics: (1) There are some things that God desires and God determines. (2) There are some things that God desires and we determine. (3) There are some things that we desire and God permits.[20] What makes life interesting—and sometimes painfully mysterious, honestly—is the interweaving of these realities. Only God himself could ever sort them out. There will always be things that we simply do not understand. But the doctrine of providence, properly understood, reassures us of God's meticulous care and ultimately good purposes. Each of these categories deserves careful consideration.

First, there are some things that God desires to happen and he sees to it that they do happen. Even a cursory glance at the design of the natural order indicates that God is a God of plan and purpose. His gift of choice to us, going back to Eden, does not nullify this fact. "People can make all kinds of plans, but only the Lord's plan will happen" (Prov. 19:21

---

[18] Hart, *Truth Aflame*, 183; adapted from Thomas C. Oden, *The Living God* (San Francisco: Harper & Row, 1987), 277–78.
[19] Jack Cottrell, *What the Bible Says About God the Ruler* (Joplin, Mo.: College Press, 1984), 304–17.
[20] I have adopted Cottrell's categories but have also adapted them. For example, my overall conception of divine providence argues for more of a meticulous involvement of God with his creation than perhaps Cottrell would see.

NCV). Isaiah, by use of a wisdom poem or poetic parable (Isa. 28:23–29),[21] reminded Israel that the Lord of hosts "is wonderful in counsel, and excellent [magnificent, NIV] in wisdom" (v. 29): He knows just how to handle every nation and mete out his judgments accordingly. Just as farmers "know how to do their work, because God has taught them" (v. 26 GNT), so God knows how to do his sovereign work: "All this wisdom comes from the Lord Almighty. The plans God makes are wise, and they always succeed" (v. 29 GNT). Psalm 33 teaches the same thing concerning God's plans and purposes (vv. 10–11):

> The LORD frustrates the purposes of the nations;
>   he keeps them from carrying out their plans.
> But his plans endure forever;
>   his purposes last eternally.

Both Isaiah (see, e.g., Isa. 14:27; 22:11; 37:26–27; 41:4; 46:10) and Jeremiah (see, e.g., Jer. 10:23; 29:11; compare Lam. 3:37–8) proclaimed that God's plans and purposes have the final say. As the apostle Paul wrote, "God always does what he plans" (Eph. 1:11 CEV).

Creation itself is something that God desired and determined to happen. The twenty-four elders in heavenly worship confessed, "for you made the whole universe; by your will, when it did not exist, it was created" (Rev. 4:11 NJB). It was God's decision alone that there would be a planet earth, populated with people made in his image. It was his sovereign decision that each of us exist. God has made many, if not most, of our decisions for us. He chose our parents, race, nationality, appearance, natural talents, and the like. His personal knowledge of each of us is astounding (Ps. 139). He has specific plans and purposes for each of our lives, which we will explore later.

Redemption is also something that God desired and determined would happen. As Peter announced on the day Pentecost, Jesus was handed over for crucifixion "according to the definite plan and foreknowledge of God" (Acts 2:23). Herod Antipas, Pontius Pilate, the Gentiles, and

---

[21] See the *Zondervan NIV Study Bible* (Grand Rapids, Mich.: Zondervan, 2002), 1072 (note on Isa. 28:23–29).

the Jews were all used by God "to do whatever your hand and your plan had predestined to take place" (Acts 4:27–28). The Bible in its entirety is an account of God's saving work on our behalf—"holy history," the scholars sometimes call it. All the myriad events recorded therein were by God's decision alone. Knowing this should fill our hearts with gratitude. We see this pattern of sovereign grace in God's dealings with Israel.

Ezekiel, for example, relates this message from God to his people:

> You say, "We want to be like the nations, like the peoples of the world, who serve wood and stone." But what you have in mind will never happen. As surely as I live, declares the Sovereign Lord, I will rule over you with a mighty hand and an outstretched arm and with outpoured wrath. I will bring you from the nations and gather you from the countries where you have been scattered—with a mighty hand and an outstretched arm and with outpoured wrath. I will bring you into the desert of the nations and there, face to face, I will execute judgment upon you. As I judged your fathers in the desert of the land of Egypt, so I will judge you, declares the Sovereign LORD. I will take note of you as you pass under my rod, and I will bring you into the bond of the covenant. I will purge you of those who revolt and rebel against me. Although I will bring them out of the land where they are living, yet they will not enter the land of Israel. Then you will know that I am the LORD (Ezek. 20:32–38 NIV[1984]).

Even today, the Jews of this world sense this sovereign choosing of God. They had no say in the matter. They have undergone tremendous suffering over the centuries just for being who they are. And as Paul reminds us, God is not through with them yet (Rom. 9–11). The same principle we see in this Ezekiel passage, however, applies to us Christians as well. Israel just wanted to blend into the surrounding cultures, but God said no. Today, we too often just want to "blend," to coast, to be laissez faire about spiritual growth. But God says, "That won't do." He is a loving parent who intends for us to "become mature, attaining to the whole measure of the fullness of Christ" (Eph. 4:13 TNIV).

Actually, we should learn to celebrate these sovereign divine decisions. In heaven we will be able to thank the Lord for making these decisions for us—that we would exist, have the parents we did, have the basic personality type he gave us, have the background, heritage, and talents he chose for us, and so forth. Further, only then will we fully appreciate the myriad ways that our Father providentially ordered our lives, even though there were so many things over which we had little or no control. Spiritual maturity in part entails that we learn the hard lesson that God is willing to work in an imperfect world, through imperfect people, to accomplish his sovereign purposes. After all, since the fall, that is all he has had to work with!

Second, there are some things that God desires, but he allows a decision on our part. He is often very patient with us and even allows us the terrifying choice of saying no to him. Hell will be populated by such people. But his benevolent intentions are evident:

> Here is something, dear friends, which you must not forget: in the Lord's sight one day is like a thousand years and a thousand years like one day. It is not that the Lord is slow in keeping his promise, as some suppose, but that he is patient with you. It is not his will that any should be lost, but that all should come to repentance (2 Peter 3:8–9 REB).

"God our Savior," wrote Paul to Timothy, "wants all people to be saved and to come to a knowledge of the truth" (1 Tim. 2:3–4 TNIV). This is a case, as mentioned earlier, where God's will is not always done, however. Jesus lamented over Jerusalem: "Jerusalem, Jerusalem, the city that kills the prophets and stones those who are sent to it! How often I have desired to gather your children together as a hen gathers her brood under her wings, and you were not willing!" (Matt. 23:37).

Do passages such as these indicate, therefore, that God's grace can be resisted? Now I have opened Pandora's Box! And we will have to address this important question in-depth in the next chapter. But I will reveal my grass roots Baptist bias now and say that God's grace, in this sense, *can* be resisted. It is only by grace that we would ever be converted. But I often urge upon those hearing the gospel that they are in a crisis if they sense the convicting presence of the Holy Spirit. I implore them not to resist him, but to yield their lives to Christ. In that sense, I am beseeching them not to resist God's grace, in my understanding. In any event, both George Whitefield (a Calvinist) and John Wesley (an Arminian) persuaded their hearers in the same way. However, much more needs to be said and will be!

This second category, of choice, has a special application to believers. For example, God wants us to be holy: "This is the will of God, that you should be holy" (1 Thess. 4:3 REB). But how often are we indifferent to God's will in this regard? Paul exhorted the Philippians: "Work out your own salvation with fear and trembling; for it is God who is at work in you, enabling you both to will and to work for his pleasure" (Phil. 2:12-13). We work *out* what God is working *in*; we are not totally passive in the process. If this is true of our ongoing Christian life, why would it not also be true of its inception? Again, we will need to look more carefully at this question later. What should concern us here is how much we miss out on because of our willful ignorance and apathy. An entire volume could be filled enumerating what God desires for his children. Actually, that volume has already been published. It is called the Holy Bible. And in that book, James, the Lord's brother, exhorts us to be "doers of the word" and to humbly "ask" for God's grace and what we *really* need (James 1:22; 4:1-6). Then he brings the discussion back around to holiness:

> So let God work his will in you. Yell a loud *no* to the Devil and watch him scamper. Say a quiet *yes* to God and he'll be there in no time. Quit dabbling in sin. Purify your inner life. Quit playing the field. Hit bottom, and cry your eyes out. The fun and games are over. Get serious, really serious. Get down on your knees before the Master; it's the only way you'll get on your feet (James 4:7-10 The Message).

And only this authentic holiness brings true happiness.

Jesus said he wants us to have abundant life (John 10:10). He said, "Ask, and it will be given you; search, and you will find; knock and the door will be opened for you"; our Father wants to "give good things to those who ask him!" (Matt. 7:7–11). Jesus is virtually giving us a blank check! Carl Bates, former president of the Southern Baptist Convention, preached a sermon in chapel during my seminary days that I will never forget. Dr. Bates said in part, "I'm convinced that when I die and go to heaven, the first thing that God is going to say to me is 'Why didn't you let me bless you more?'" Too often we find ourselves sifting through the garbage of this world, when we could be enjoying a feast of God's best blessings for our lives. It is his will. Is it our will?

Third, there are some things that we desire and God permits. The Scriptures do teach in some sense a *permissive* will of God (Acts 14:16; 16:7; 18:21; 1 Cor. 4:19; 16:7; Heb. 6:3; James 4:13–15). "God evidently allows us a circle of freedom on certain matters of indifference."[22] In general, he does not care what brand of toothpaste we choose or which suit or dress we decide to wear. However, even in mundane matters he might choose to give direction. Early in his ministry, Pat Robertson felt impressed one morning to wear a certain tie. On his plane flight the gentleman sitting next to him commented on the tie, which led to a conversation in which Robertson had the opportunity of leading the man to the Lord! The smallest details of our lives matter to God. At the same time, we are his children, not his puppets. We need not be obsessive in these matters, agonizing in prayer over the type of deodorant we should buy. Our greatest freedom in life comes in yielding the reins to God and finding his peace and power through surrender to his will.

Guidance

But precisely how do we discern God's will in the swirl of life that surrounds us? How can we better cooperate with God's providential

---
[22] Hart, *Truth Aflame*, 185.

workings in our life? I have found that there are basically five ways in which God's will is communicated to us: faith, facts, feelings, friends, and fences. We will look at each of these in turn. But before doing so, it would be helpful to consider the *model* that we have (perhaps even unconsciously) as to how God works out his will in our lives.

Many people think of God's plan for our lives as a rigid blueprint that he lays out in eternity. One wrong move, one bad decision, and we're cursed with second best the rest of our lives. Common sense tells us this is an impossible model. For it to work, our parents before us (and their parents before them in an infinite regress) would have had to follow God's blueprint for their individual lives perfectly, including choosing the right mate, for us to get started right in following our own blueprint.

It is better to think of God as more like a master chess player. We are making many decisions in authentic freedom, but he is a million moves ahead of us, and knows easily how to get us where he wants us. He influences us in countless subtle ways, and he weaves all the tangled threads of our lives into a beautiful tapestry—even our mistakes and failures. Grace means that even a failed marriage or a fatal business decision is never final. We can get right back on the right path and move ahead. All of us have done that in a thousand different ways anyway!

> There are basically five ways in which God's will is communicated to us: faith, facts, feelings, friends, and fences.

But we all know how damaging careless decision-making can be in our lives. And we all desire to make quality life decisions rooted in God's plans and purposes. How do we do it? I want to lay out five ways that God guides his children. When these avenues of divine guidance dovetail, we can have assurance that we are walking in God's will and discovering our divine design. The first principle of divine guidance is the most fundamental: faith.

"The just shall live by faith" (Rom. 1:17 NKJV). "Trust in the Lord with all your heart, and do not rely on your own insight. In all your ways acknowledge him [lit. know him], and he will make straight your paths [lit. he will clear your path; compare CEV: 'he will clear the road for you to follow']" (Prov. 3:5–6); "for we walk by faith, not by sight" (2 Cor. 5:7). Programmatic passages like these powerfully express the faith principle. God expects us to live by faith, by daily trusting in and relying upon him: "And without faith it is impossible to please God" (Heb. 11:6).

The Christian faith pilgrimage begins with a decisive faith commitment of our lives to God:

> I appeal to you therefore, brothers and sisters, by the mercies of God, to present your bodies as a living sacrifice, holy and acceptable to God, which is your spiritual worship. Do not be conformed to this world, but be transformed by the renewing of your minds, so that you may discern what is the will of God—what is good and acceptable and perfect (Rom. 12:1–2).

First comes the *consecration* ("present your bodies as a living sacrifice"), then comes the *revelation* ("so that you may discern what is the will of God"). Too often we want a revelation of God's will *so that we can decide whether we want to do it!* But God says no. First, we make a no-strings-attached commitment of our lives. Then comes the discernment of God's will.

We have to be willing to walk by faith, like our father Abraham, who had to launch out on the Lord's promise of a land he had never seen (Gen. 12:1). Job had to trust God even when he was enduring all of Satan's afflictions. The greatest faith entails learning to trust God even when we don't understand what is happening in our lives. The essence of the Christian life is learning to trust. Faith means humble dependence upon God for literally *everything.* It is acknowledging to our Lord that without him we can do nothing (John 15:5). It is a covenant commitment and consecration of our lives. But there is more. We also need the guidance of God's Word.

The Bible is divine revelation. It is literally the Word of God. It is the authoritative, inspired, infallible, and inerrant Word of God. That cannot be said of any other book! When God gave us his Word through the supernatural influence of the Holy Spirit upon the biblical writers, he gave it as a revelation of his will. The writers were inspired as well as the writings themselves. The Bible is a God-breathed book:

> All Scripture is God-breathed and is useful for teaching the truth, rebuking error, correcting faults, and giving instruction for right living, so that the person who serves God may be fully equipped for every good work (2 Tim. 3:16, compare NIV, GNT, NRSV).

The term translated "God-breathed" means that the Bible was "breathed out by God" (ESV). The Bible is the direct result of the breath (Spirit) and speech (Word) of God. It is the Word of God.

The Bible did not have "its origin in the human will, but prophets, though human, spoke from God as they were carried along by the Holy Spirit" (2 Peter 1:21 TNIV). The word translated "carried along by" suggests the picture of a ship being carried along by the wind across the waters. So both the writings (2 Tim. 3:16) and the writers (2 Peter 1:20, 21) were inspired as God gave us his authoritative Word. In the final analysis, every word of the Bible is God's Word.

At least 95% of God's will for our lives is already revealed in the Bible. The question then becomes, "If we are not troubling ourselves to learn and do his will as it has already been revealed in the Bible, why should God entrust us with that other 5% of his personalized plans for each of our lives? God's Word is a lamp to our feet and a light to our path (Ps. 119:105). Have we availed ourselves of that light? "How can young people keep their way pure? By guarding it according to your word" (Ps. 119:9). Are we guarding our way according to God's Word?

I once heard a preacher ask a congregation, "How many of you believe everything you read in the newspaper?" No one raised a hand. He then inquired, "How many of you believe everything you read in the Bible?" Just about everyone raised a hand. Then he asked, "Then why do you spend more time every day reading something you can't always believe than you do something you can always believe?"

> At least 95% of God's will for our lives is already revealed in the Bible.

I have never met an overcoming Christian who did not have a rich knowledge of and daily life in God's Word. But I have met plenty of frustrated, confused, and defeated Christians who did not have this knowledge of and relationship with the Bible. We should read the Bible so much that our blood is bibline!

So often God will personalize to us a biblical passage, which is just what we need for the day! It's like daily manna. We live by the Word. Jesus said that we need "every word that comes from the mouth of God" (Matt. 4:4). We should read through the Bible at least once each year for a broad exposure to the whole counsel of God, and there are many wonderful Bibles and reading plans available to guide us. But we should also study the Scriptures (preferably in the fellowship of the church). Finally, we should read the Scriptures meditatively and devotionally for soul nourishment. However, we need to be careful that we aren't tempted to read the Bible as some kind of magic book for guidance.

One person decided just to open the Bible at random to get his marching orders for the day. He read, "Judas went out and hanged himself." He didn't particularly like that one, so he opened the Bible again and read, "Go thou, and do likewise." Now he was really concerned, so he tried one more time: "What thou doest, do quickly." He learned his lesson. People have made some weird decisions using this method. And even the devil himself can quote (and twist) scripture!

However, there may indeed be those times when a particular passage leaps out at us, and it is crystal clear that God is communicating something very personal and precious to us. It is one of the pearls of having a life in the Word. The Scriptures are "the sword of the Spirit" (Eph. 6:17), and through them God enables us to discern the true "thoughts and intentions" of our hearts (Heb. 4:12). God can do spiritual surgery on our hearts as we read his Word! He can also personalize pertinent promises to us in our times of need.

Vision is imparted as we read the Bible as well. God has clearly revealed his vision and agenda for his people. But too often we try to derive our own and bring confusion into our lives. The Great Commandment and the Great Commission are the universal marching orders for Gods' people. The Great Commandment teaches us to love God with our whole being and to love our neighbor as ourselves (Mark 12:29–31). And in his Great Commission Jesus states:

> All authority in heaven and on earth has been given to me. Go therefore and make disciples of all nations, baptizing them in the name of the Father and of the Son and of the Holy Spirit, and teaching them to obey everything that I have commanded you. And remember, I am with you always, to the end of the age (Matt. 28:18–20).

That is why we are on this planet. All of our personal goals and plans must fit into this overall divine agenda.[23]

Adapting Rick Warren's slogan to our purposes in this book, we could say:

> A great commitment
> To our glorious Christ
> And his Great Commandment
> And his Great Commission
> Makes a great Christian
> And a great Church!

---

[23] See Rick Warren's two classics: *The Purpose-Driven Church* (Grand Rapids, Mich.: Zondervan, 1995) and *The Purpose-Driven Life* (Grand Rapids, Mich.: Zondervan, 2002).

So we must learn to trust, and we must learn the truth. We need the real facts of life as revealed in God's Word. But we must also learn to be sensitive to the promptings of the Holy Spirit.

Every true believer has the Holy Spirit (Rom. 8:9), but not every believer has learned to listen to the Holy Spirit and to be more fully led by him. "For all who are led by the Spirit of God are children of God" (Rom. 8:14). "Since we live by the Spirit, let us keep in step with the Spirit" (Gal. 5:25 NIV). "And let the peace of Christ rule in your hearts" (Col. 3:15). We *can* have the personal guidance of God's Spirit in our lives. But the honest question of many is: How?

The Holy Spirit's communication to us is both objective and subjective. His objective communication is found, of course, in his Word, the Bible. His subjective communication is Spirit-to-spirit—God's Holy Spirit to our human spirit. However, our minds are involved as well. He may bring a scripture or message spontaneously to mind in a strategic moment in our decision process. He may provide simply a strong impression about a given action's wisdom. We lose our peace when we are straying off course and have a tremendous peace and joy when we are on course. A wise pastor once taught me that we must give *expression* to God's *impressions*. The more we get into this habit of obedience, the stronger the Spirit's impressions will become. The less we do so, the more insensitive we become and the communication is garbled.

> A wise pastor once taught me that we must give expression to God's impressions. The more we get into this habit of obedience, the stronger the Spirit's impressions will become.

During my college years I sold vacuum cleaners door-to-door. I had two goals in mind: (1) to witness to the lost and (2) to sell vacuum cleaners. Neither was happening initially, so I got desperate: I prayed!

I felt impressed to drive to the opposite side of town. Looking down a street to my right, when I got there, I saw a plowed field at the end of the street. Joy began to leap in my heart. I knew God had something prepared for me—the soil had already been prepared! I went to the first house and rang the doorbell. When the lady answered, I said, "Hi, I'm selling vacuum cleaners—you need one?" That's exactly the wrong question to ask. Everyone already has a vacuum cleaner. But the nice lady said, "As a matter of fact, we just bought new carpet. And last night my husband told me that I could get a new vacuum cleaner, if I wanted to."

I knew I had a sale, but what about the witnessing opportunity? I went in to demonstrate my marvelous machine and noticed a wonderful Christian book on her coffee table. "Have you read that book?" I asked. She replied, "Oh, yes! In fact, I only recently became a Christian and was baptized." Then she added, "Say, could you come back tonight, show the machine to my husband, and witness to him? I've really been praying for him!"

All of this happened because I gave *expression* to God's *impression*. There was something in my gut that said, "Go there; God's got something ready for you." And marvelous ministry took place! *And* I sold a vacuum cleaner and made a little money—which every college student can appreciate! Following the Spirit's promptings is an exciting adventure. It is an art that we learn over the years. And we can sometimes miss it.

Martin Luther was debating some heretics who claimed the Spirit's revelation for their false, unbiblical teachings. Luther kept saying, "But the Bible says…" and his opponents kept saying, "The Spirit! The Spirit!" Finally, in exasperation, Luther said, "I slap your spirit in the snout!" He knew that the *Holy Spirit* would never "reveal" a teaching contrary to God's Word.

David Yonggi Cho, the pastor of the world's largest church, was asked what his secret of success was. He said simply, "I pray and I obey." That *is* the secret! Sin always hardens our hearts. Obedience by the Spirit keeps our hearts tender and sensitive. Humble, dependent prayer and a lifestyle of sensitive obedience to the Spirit's promptings will clear the path for us![24] But we should also be open to the counsel of others. They too can be instruments of the Spirit in providing wisdom and insight in life's decisions.

God often uses *friends* to guide us. The Bible says, "Without counsel, plans go wrong, but with many advisers they succeed" (Prov. 15:22). As the church we are "one body in Christ, and individually we are members of one another" (Rom. 12:5). And we really need each other (1 Cor. 12:14–26)! The counsel of trusted friends with a proven walk in the Lord is priceless. We are foolish to deprive ourselves of this God-ordained resource. However, people cannot make decisions for us. A sure sign of spiritual immaturity is the tendency to cling to others, continually asking for advice with the goal of their making decisions for us. I am amazed, nonetheless, at how many times God has used others to help me along the right path.

I was newly married and beginning my doctoral work in seminary. One day my wife came to me in tears. She is not one to cry that readily, so I was immediately concerned. She told me that while she was in college, God seemed to be using her consistently in effective ministry. She was an active member in Campus Crusade for Christ and in her local church. Now she found herself in a routine of going to work as a rehabilitation counselor and going to services at the church where I was serving as an associate pastor. Our lifestyle was hectic, and she felt that God had "put her on the shelf," as it were, in terms of fruitful ministry. At a worship service the next evening, a lay witness team was sharing. An elderly gentleman stepped to the microphone and explained a ministry that he and a middle-aged lady on the team had. While we were singing, he would see mental pictures as he looked out over the congregation, and the lady would interpret their significance. I was dressed casually and seated out in the pews with my wife. There was no way that these two people would know that I was a preacher and on the ministerial

---

[24] More will be said about prayer below.

staff of the church. The older gentleman said, "For example, I saw that young man there," pointing to me. "He had a pile of boomerangs beside him. He would pick one up and hand it to that young lady beside him. She would do something with the boomerang, smoothing off the rough edges or something, and then hand it back to him. Then he would throw out the boomerang. Then they would repeat the process." The woman said, "That young man has a ministry in the Word of God, and God has called that young lady alongside him to smooth off the rough edges of his preaching and teaching ministry. And the boomerangs stand for the Word of God that never returns void." Needless to say, my wife and I were touched and encouraged.

Years later, in Tulsa, Oklahoma, we had been meeting in prayer for months with a group of people seeking guidance about whether to plant a new church in the city. Tulsa has more churches than people, and I often said, "Tulsa doesn't need another church." Yet, the growing conviction was that we should start the church. Earlier my wife and I had had the privilege of taking a group of seven seminary students to Argentina to work with the ministry of Omar Cabrera, who had established a string of churches in Argentina with about 170,000 people. Now Cabrera was in Tulsa, speaking on the campus where I teach. I prayed on the way that God might further confirm his guidance about planting the new church. The dean of the seminary, who was the one who had originally asked us to pray about starting the church (to whom I had responded, "Tulsa doesn't need another church"), was seated toward the front of the auditorium. My wife and I were seated toward the back. Cabrera talked for about an hour on the theme of not letting your natural mind talk you out of God's will. "For example," he said, "you may be praying about starting a new church in Tulsa, but your natural mind is saying, 'Tulsa doesn't need another church.' You shouldn't let your natural mind talk you out of God's will." The dean turned at that point and smiled at me. I immediately thought that the dean and Omar had already been talking about this prospect. The next day, I called Omar and asked him.

He laughed and told me that the dean had asked him the same question about me. He knew nothing about our previous conversations. He said, "Brother, I believe the Lord wants you to start that church." We did, and it grew to about 250 people very quickly. It is still a vital church.

God also uses *fences* or circumstances to guide us. Twice the apostle Paul made reference to God's opening a door for him: "for a wide door for effective work has opened to me, and there are many adversaries (1 Cor. 16:9); "a door was opened for me in the Lord" (2 Cor. 2:12). The Lord's message to the church in Philadelphia contained in part these words: "Look, I have set before you an open door, which no one is able to shut" (Rev. 3:8). God can open a door that no one can shut and shut a door that no one can open. However, too often we depend solely on circumstances for guidance, forgetting that there can be "many adversaries" and adversities involved in doing God's will. Too often we resign rather that resist when encountering difficulties in our Christian lives and service. Christianity is a "good fight" (2 Tim. 4:7). And it is a good fight because through Christ we win!

When faith, facts, feelings, friends, and fences dovetail, we can be assured of clear guidance from God. Prayer has emerged as a relevant subject in all these discussions as well. It too plays a vital role in God's providence and merits further exploration.

Prayer

Prayer is so abundant in the Bible that it could be called a prayer book.[25] Both Testaments are replete with prayer. Prayer is at the heart of a living faith, giving expression to the *relationship* between God and his people in the ongoing pilgrimage to heaven. The purpose of this brief concluding section will be to reflect on the meaning of prayer within the overall context of the gracious providential dealings of God with his creation.

---

[25] See Hart, *Truth Aflame*, 188–93.

Never is maintaining the balance between immanence and transcendence more crucial than in deriving a theology of prayer. Imbalance toward transcendence can turn prayer into "mental pushups"—something we do to better ourselves, but having no real effect beyond psychological health. Imbalance toward immanence can turn God into a warm and fuzzy feeling or a divine Santa Claus, who exists primarily to meet our needs and desires. Those who think seriously about the meaning of prayer can inadvertently make prayer a problem: If God already knows what is going to happen, already knows what we are going to pray, then does prayer really make a difference? Does prayer change things? Does prayer ever change God's mind? Does prayer ever bring miracles?

As with guidance, the *model* we adopt, whether consciously or unconsciously, influences our understanding and practice of prayer profoundly. If prayer is an interchange between God and humanity, then can our prayers change God's mind? The answer is yes and no. From the vantage point of God's eternal transcendence, nothing takes God by surprise, and his knowledge of the future is comprehensive. He knows literally everything that will transpire in the future. From the vantage point of God's immanence, however, we have an entirely different picture. Throughout the Scriptures, we see God interacting with us and changing his mind in response to our intercessions and petitions. Leonard Sweet would call this a "double ring" truth, which postmoderns seem to revel in. Those pressing for linear logic here, however, will only be frustrated. It is helpful to follow this analogy as it relates to other biblical doctrines.

Jesus Christ is God incarnate. How shall we go about conceptualizing this reality? If we begin "from above," in terms of his heavenly origins, we may compromise the authenticity of his humanity. If we begin from below, we may lose sight of his heavenly origins, his *preexistence* as the eternal Son of God. That is the story of much of contemporary Christology. We have to affirm both dimensions simultaneously.

The same is true of the Trinity. If we begin with God's threeness, we may never arrive at his oneness and consequently turn him into a committee God of three finite beings. If we begin with God's oneness, we may never be able to extrapolate his threeness and end up with a unitarianian concept of God. Rather, we must affirm both realities simultaneously—three in one, one in three.

Conceptualizing prayer requires holding the heavenly and earthly perspectives together. If you think of God solely in transcendent terms, then he becomes the "unmoved mover" of philosophy and your prayer life suffers. If you lose that dimension, however, God becomes a finite being—sorely limited, even pathetic—who can do little or nothing in response to your prayers. Thus, there are both theoretical and practical implications to our model of prayer. Did God take a risk in bringing forth such a creation? If we have anything resembling authentic choice in life, then surely there is risk involved—certainly, but on *our* part, not God's. Returning to our model and overall doctrine of God, if God has no limits on his knowledge and power, then nothing ever takes him by surprise and he truly can *see ahead and provide what is needed* to achieve his holy, loving purposes. That is the essence of what we mean by providence. On our side things are different, however.

We are finite, imperfect creatures. Even the saintliest among us must admit to mistakes and imperfections. Further, we all are painfully aware of bad decisions in our lives and the often destructive results which followed. But there is also a more positive way to look at this situation. Evidently, God intended our lives to be a great adventure, with unknown and unexpected challenges and problems along with an exciting prospect of achieving—solely by God's common and special grace—ultimate meaning and eternal bliss. In that sense, risk is good. Risk on our part is *right*, as John Piper cogently argues.[26]

---

[26] See John Piper, *Don't Waste Your Life* (Wheaton, Ill.: Crossway Books, 2003), 79–98.

Therefore, common grace and providence, rightly conceived and perceived, provide us with a sense of security, meaning, and adventure. We become the freest people on the planet! Even in the darkest hours of our lives, there runs deep within a river of joy and peace. But beyond this common grace lies a special, saving, miracle-making grace that truly sets apart the life of a believer. It is to this greatest of all realities—the *actuality* of a God of all grace who redeems and transforms every dimension of our lives, a God who takes us all the way to glory!—that we must now turn.

> Common grace and providence, rightly conceived and perceived, provide us with a sense of security, meaning, and adventure. We become the freest people on the planet!

Chapter Six:
Special Grace

SPECIAL GRACE IS SAVING GRACE. It is that "amazing grace" that Christians have celebrated for centuries. Special grace, like special revelation, involves a holy land, a holy people, and a holy book.[1] It is *historical* (objective) in nature. God walked across the pages of history on a saving mission. The Bible is the inspired account of that journey. He raised up the nation of Israel as a light to the nations and brought forth from them the Savior of the world, Jesus Christ. And this Jesus the Messiah, Jesus of Nazareth, was ultimately found to be none other than God himself enfleshed. He was the human face of God. He went to the cross to purchase eternal redemption for us, rose from the dead, and comes personally into our lives through the Holy Spirit. Thus, saving grace is also *personal* (subjective). It points to God's invasion of our lives. He makes our entire being his residence. He forms us into a supernatural body known as the church and sends us out on mission to spread this good news to the world.

Therefore, special grace is a very *concrete* reality. The eastern end of the Mediterranean is called the Holy Land because that is where God's saving revelation took place. Any saint who has had the privilege of visiting there knows even more profoundly why this truly is holy ground. In addition, God has always had a people. Jews and Christians are flesh and blood human beings with whom God has had special dealings down through history for saving purposes. And the Bible is a holy book because it is God's book. We believe in its authority, inspiration, infallibility, and inerrancy. We generally put the words "Holy Bible" on its cover. Between its covers is the story of God's amazing grace. Thus, special grace is more than a concept. It has both objective and subjective

---
[1] Larry D. Hart, *Truth Aflame* (Grand Rapids, Mich.: Zondervan, 2005), 46–48.

dimensions to it. It is God's sending his Son into history and sending the Spirit of his Son into our hearts (Gal. 4:4–7).

Special grace points to the astounding truth of a gracious God who takes the initiative in preparing us to receive his gift of salvation. It refers as well to specifically how he rescues us, transforms us, and keeps us savingly in his care. It encompasses a significant number of "kinds" of grace, although there has never been a consensus as to exactly how many there may be. We will delineate several in the discussion to follow. It is helpful to obtain a bird's-eye view of grace in general before launching into an analysis of special grace in particular.

The Three Dimensions of Grace

There are three fundamental *dimensions* to grace as seen in the Scriptures. Grace in the Bible refers first of all to the *attributes of God*. Grace is a divine attribute closely related to other attributes such as love, mercy, and goodness. In fact, grace as an attribute can be subsumed under the general rubric of love. "The LORD, the LORD, a God merciful and gracious, slow to anger, and abounding in steadfast love and faithfulness" (Ex. 34:6). He is "the God of all grace" (1 Peter 5:10). Ironically, it was only because of God's response to our *sin* that we were able to see both his wrath and his loving grace, mercy, and patience. Only fallen and redeemed humanity can fully appreciate God's attribute of grace.

Further, grace in the Bible points to the *activities of God* in both common and special grace. In the previous chapter on common grace we glimpsed the myriad ways that God provides for his creation. He governs and preserves the universe, which is truly a variegated enterprise! If he left merely one of these responsibilities to us,—for example, feeding all the birds of this world—we would learn very quickly to appreciate all that he is *doing*. But special grace is even more spectacular—in fact, infinitely so. Why Holy God would ever stoop to rescue sinful humanity will always amaze us! Paul gave Titus this programmatic statement concerning special grace:

For the grace of God has appeared that offers salvation to all people. It teaches us to say "No" to ungodliness and worldly passions, and to live self-controlled, upright and godly lives in this present age, while we wait for the blessed hope—the appearing of the glory of our great God and Savior, Jesus Christ, who gave himself for us to redeem us from all wickedness and to purify for himself a people that are his very own, eager to do what is good (Titus 2:11–14 TNIV).

It is this saving grace that is the primary focus of this chapter. But there is another dimension of grace to which we will devote a separate chapter: grace as the *attitudes and actions of God's people*. But before we become God's people and begin to live out this grace, we must receive the special grace which "offers salvation to all people."

The Power of God

"I am not ashamed of the gospel," Paul wrote the Romans, "because it is the power of God that brings salvation to everyone who believes: first to the Jew, then to the Gentile" (Rom. 1:16 TNIV). Paul had experienced the *power* of the gospel first hand and was certainly personally aware of how "the grace of our Lord" had "overflowed" for him (1 Tim. 1:14). He repeatedly reminded the Ephesians that we are all saved by this powerful grace (Eph. 2:1–10). As we saw earlier in our study of the biblical theology of grace, special grace is the *power* of God in action on our behalf. It is the power of God's Spirit, applying the saving work of Christ and bringing deliverance to people. "With great power the apostles gave their testimony to the resurrection of the Lord Jesus, and great grace was upon them all" (Acts 4:33). "Stephen, full of grace

> Special grace is the power of God in action on our behalf. It is the power of God's Spirit, applying the saving work of Christ and bringing deliverance to people.

and power, did great wonders and signs among the people" (Acts 6:8). James D. G. Dunn summarizes Paul's concept of grace in this regard quite well: "For Paul grace means *power*, an otherly power at work in and through the believer's life, the *experience* of God's Spirit."[2] Thus, our salvation is totally the work of the powerful grace of God. In our fallenness we would never have the inclination to seek after God. Only because of his grace are we drawn to him and receive the gift of life abundant and eternal.

Prevenient Grace

One particular theological term has become associated with the preparing work of God's Spirit, as he woos us unto himself, drawing our interest, convicting us of sin, and enabling us to repent. The broad topic of consideration here is what has come to be known as *prevenient grace* or *preventing grace*. Thomas Oden writes:

> Prevening grace antecedes human responsiveness so as to prepare the soul for the effective hearing of the redeeming Word. This preceding grace draws persons closer to God, lessens their blindness to divine remedies, strengthens their will to accept revealed truth, and enables repentance. Only when sinners are assisted by prevenient grace can they begin to yield their hearts to cooperation with subsequent forms of grace.[3]

Oden cites Augustine and Aquinas as teaching this concept. Whether one accepts a Calvinistic or an Arminian perspective, the view is the same in regard to the priority of grace. God takes the initiative in our salvation. "That is the whole point of grace: it does not start with us, it starts with God," says Philip Edgcumbe Hughes, when defining prevenient grace.[4]

---

[2] James D. G. Dunn, *Jesus and the Spirit: A Study of the Religious and Charismatic Experience of Jesus and the First Christians as Reflected in the New Testament* (London: SCM Press, 1975, 202–03.
[3] Thomas C. Oden, *The Transforming Power of Grace* (Nashville: Abingdon Press, 1993), 47.
[4] Philip Edgcumbe Hughes, "Grace" in *Evangelical Dictionary of Theology*, ed. Walter A. Elwell (Grand Rapids, Mich.: Baker, 1984), 480.

It was while we were "still powerless," "still sinners," and "God's enemies" that he gave us salvation through Christ (Rom. 5:6–11 TNIV). God's love is always prior. "In this is love, not that we loved God but that he loved us and sent his Son to be the atoning sacrifice for our sins" (1 John 4:10). "We love," John writes, "because he first loved us" (v. 19). We were spiritually dead and "by nature children of wrath" when God saved us by his grace (Eph. 2:1–10). The spiritual reality being referred to here is that convicting and convincing work of the Holy Spirit (John 16:8–11). This is one of the greatest evidences for the reality of God.

I first experienced this work of the Holy Spirit as a six-year-old. Looking back, it is difficult for me now to fathom how a child so young could experience such a dramatic conversion. I have had a drive to know God for as long as I can remember myself. My mother was born again on October 13, 1946. Three months later she found out that I was on the way. She immediately dedicated me to the Lord. I was born on October 13, 1947, the one year anniversary of her spiritual birth. That is special grace at work! And it is obvious that God was preparing the way—even before I was born. The Holy Spirit, like John the Baptist, prepares the way for the Savior to enter our lives. God knows precisely what he is doing, and his grace is truly effective.

Sufficient Grace

Just as the apostle Paul learned that God's grace was sufficient for him to be able to deal with his thorn in the flesh and that God's power was perfected in Paul's weakness (2 Cor. 12:7–10), so special grace is seen to be *sufficient grace* when it comes to salvation for all people. Sufficient grace points us to: (1) the *calling* of special grace and (2) the *competence* of special grace.

Both John the Baptist and Jesus began their ministries with a call to repentance.[5] Matthew seems to take a personal interest in this calling of special grace. He notes how Jesus called Peter and Andrew, then James and

---
[5] John the Baptist: Matt. 3:1–12; Mark 1:1–8; Luke 3:1–20; Jesus: Matt. 4:12–17; Mark 1:14–15.

John, on Lake Galilee, to follow him and fish for people (Matt. 4:18–22; compare Mark 1:16–20; Luke 5:1–11; John 1:40–42). He further relates his own calling (Matt. 9:9–13; compare Mark 2:13–17; Luke 5:27–32). He notes how Jesus warned the unrepentant cities of Chorazin, Bethsaida, and Capernaum of judgment for ignoring his gracious deeds of power (Matt. 11:20–24; compare Luke 10:12–15). Then, Matthew alone relates Jesus' unforgettable words of invitation familiar to many:

> Come to me, all you that are weary and are carrying heavy burdens, and I will give you rest. Take my yoke upon you, and learn from me; for I am gentle and humble in heart, and you will find rest for your souls. For my yoke is easy, and my burden is light (Matt. 11:28–29).

It was a call to salvation, sanctification (discipleship), and service.[6] Matthew makes it clear that Jesus intended this gospel invitation to be proclaimed throughout the world (Matt. 24:14; 28:18–20).

Matthew also relates a kingdom parable of Jesus in which the call to a king's wedding banquet for his son is met with various responses (Matt. 22:1–14). Some are indifferent (v. 5), some overtly rebellious (v. 6), and some self-righteous (vv. 11–12).[7] Everyone, "both good and bad," are invited in order to fill the wedding hall (vv. 8–10). None of the original invitees made it the banquet (v. 8). But there was even one individual who showed up but was thrown out because he did not have the proper attire (vv. 11–13). "One may not stand before God unprepared for judgment and expect to presume upon his grace"; these are "the would-be disciples who fail to 'count the cost'" (compare Jesus' great dinner parable in Luke [Luke 14:15–24] and the follow-up on counting the cost [vv. 25–33]).[8] These could well be the self-righteous Jewish opponents who plotted to entrap Jesus and lynch him (Matt. 22:15–23:39). Jesus' final statement in this parable deserves careful notice: "Many are called, but few are chosen" (Matt. 22:14).

---

[6] *Ryrie Study Bible*, expanded ed. (Chicago: Moody Press, 1995), 1532 (note on Matt. 11:28–30).
[7] See *Ryrie Study Bible*, 1,555 (note on Matt. 22:14).
[8] Craig L. Blomberg, *Interpreting the Parables* (Downers Grove, Ill.: InterVarsity Press 1990), 237–40.

The call goes out to all, but only those who accept the call are the chosen. In one of his earliest letters the apostle Paul reminds his recent converts that "God has chosen you for salvation through sanctification by the Spirit and through belief in the truth. He called you to this through our gospel, so that you might obtain the glory of our Lord Jesus Christ" (2 Thess. 2:13–14 HCSB). According to Paul, believers are "called to belong to Jesus Christ" and "called to be saints" (Rom. 1:6–7).[9] Those of us who love God are "called according to his purpose" (Rom. 8:28). Paul goes on to speak of the predestination, justification, and glorification of those who are called, for whom everything works together for good (vv. 28–30). To those who are "the called," Paul wrote the Corinthians, Christ is "the power of God and the wisdom of God" (1 Cor. 1:24).

The call of God goes out through the preaching of the gospel. The preaching of the message of the cross, of Christ crucified, seems foolish to those who are perishing. It is scandalous to the Jews and moronic to the Gentiles, but to those being saved it is the power of God (1 Cor. 1:18–26). People need one thing more than any other: They need to hear the gospel of Jesus Christ. "And how are they to hear without a preacher?" (Rom. 10:14 RSV). We are saved by "hearing about Christ and having faith in him" (Gal. 3:2 CEV). "No one can have faith without hearing the message about Christ" (Rom. 10:17 CEV). As Paul reminded Titus, God promised us eternal life, and he "never lies" (Titus 1:2): "At the right time God let the world know about that life through preaching. He trusted me with that work, and I preached by the command of God our Savior" (v. 3 NCV). Thus, Paul links the call to salvation specifically to preaching.

The Lord does the calling: Special, saving grace comes to "everyone whom the Lord our God calls to him" (Acts 2:39). But the Lord expects

> The call of God goes out through the preaching of the gospel.

---
[9] Literally, "called of Jesus Christ" and "called saints" (compare 1 Cor. 1:2).

us, in response, to "call on him" (Rom. 10:12). "For 'Everyone who calls on the name of the Lord shall be saved'" (v. 13, quoting Joel 2:32). We may never fully fathom why some, having heard the gospel, refuse to respond. But in the most profound sense, that is God's business anyway, not ours. Our business is to herald the good news of God's saving grace around the globe, and to pray that the Lord would send out even more laborers into the harvest (Matt. 9:37–38). And we can go in the confidence that God's sovereign grace will accomplish its purposes.

A consideration of the *calling* of special grace leads very naturally into the encouraging truth of the *competence* of special grace. This is usually referred to by theologians as effective (or efficacious, effectual) grace. God's grace is obviously sufficient for the salvation of all people, but only those who actually receive this special grace experience effective grace.[10] Paul was only hurting himself as he fought against God "like an ox kicking against its owner's stick" (Acts 26:14 GNT). Later he would see that God had set him apart *before he was born* "and called me through his grace" (Gal. 1:15).[11] God had sovereign purposes in mind for Paul, one of which was to make him "an example to those who would come to believe in [Jesus Christ] for eternal life" (1 Tim. 1:16). Paul had supreme confidence in God's keeping power over his life and ministry (2 Tim. 1:12). Thus, Paul would see God's competent grace as a *conquering* grace and a *preserving* grace. But this same apostle, in his portrayal of special grace, also raises important questions for us, which have yet to be fully addressed. He writes of a sovereign *election* and *predestination* of true believers. Precisely what did he mean to communicate by such terms?

Election and Predestination

The apostle Peter was right: There are some things in Paul's letters which are "hard to understand" (2 Peter 3:16)! One thing is certain, and

---

[10] Hughes, "Grace," 482.
[11] See Hughes, "Grace," 481. Hughes and I may use some terminology somewhat differently, but, as far as I can tell, we share a common vision of special grace.

that is that the church has yet to reach a consensus on what Paul intended to say about such matters as election and predestination. Even Calvin, as we shall see, cautioned about how we should go about teaching such truths. And it is Calvin's views as such in this arena which have often been the storm center of debates about special grace. To part company over honest differences of opinion, however, would be to violate the very grace that Paul was defending (more about this in the last chapter). It is precisely at this point that theological method becomes all-important.

Calvin included his distinctive treatment of these topics in his *Institutes* simply because he saw them in the Scriptures and wanted to include them in his soteriology (not his doctrine of God). Calvin's followers, however, have sometimes made predestination the rational principle for an entire systematic theology. And distortion inevitably follows from that methodology. Perhaps the best place to begin is with a previously mentioned Pauline passage: Romans 8:28–30.

> We know that all things work together for good for those who love God, who are called according to his purpose. For those whom he foreknew he also predestined to be conformed to the image of his Son, in order that he might be the firstborn within a large family [or among many brothers and sisters]. And those whom he predestined he also called; and those whom he called he also justified; and those whom he justified he also glorified.

The first portion of this passage is widely known and very popular. But with the mention of such concepts as foreknowledge and predestination the atmosphere too often changes into theological wrangle. Apart from the perennial disputes over the precise nature of predestination, the concept of divine foreknowledge is presently the most hotly contested topic. The doctrine of God is in purview here, however, whereas our focus in this study is on grace. Are the doctrines of divine foreknowledge and predestination grace doctrines? The answer is an unqualified yes.

What exactly did Paul mean by "those whom he foreknew" (Rom. 8:29)? The first thing to be clarified is the nature of God's knowledge as it is portrayed in the Scriptures. God's knowledge is consistently depicted in the Bible as a *loving* knowledge. God's knowledge of us is an intimate, personal, affectionate knowledge. For example, the Bible says that Adam "knew his wife Eve," which obviously means more than they had a nice friendship, for the very next words are, "and she conceived" (Gen. 4:1). In the classic Psalm 139, David begins: "O LORD, you have searched me and known me" (v. 1). The entire psalm is an amazing portrait of God and his infinite knowledge and love for his creatures. Therefore, our first instinct should be to think of the *love* of God when we read the words, "those whom he foreknew." The concept of an *electing* love cannot be precluded either (Gen. 18:19; Jer. 1:5; Amos 3:2).[12] God "knows," that is, chooses his servants. But is there more? There is good reason not to preclude the concept of simple cognition in God's foreknowledge.

We have already read how Christ's crucifixion took place "according to the definite plan and foreknowledge of God" (Act 2:23). The Scriptures are crystal clear that God's knowledge of the future is complete and perfect. In fact, he defends his own deity in part on that knowledge (in contrast to all the false gods). Isaiah is replete with passages carrying this argument. Bruce Ware provides us with an edifying and convincing treatment of such passages in his *God's Lesser Glory*, a devastating critique of open theism: Isaiah 41:21–29; 42:8–9; 43:8–13; 44:6–8; 44:24–28; 45:1–7, 18–25; 46:8–11; and 48:3–8.[13] Therefore, it would not necessarily be in error at all to include the idea that God's predestination is predicated on his foreknowledge of our future free decisions. That is one of the first topics of debate in relation to the concept of predestination.

Now we are hearing the two prevailing leitmotifs of the Christian symphony of grace! One emphasizes the sovereignty and glory of God. The other highlights the freedom and responsibility of humanity. The two must be kept together. And it takes the grace of God to do so! Calvinists will only hear the note of election in the term "foreknew." Here is a

---

[12] See C. E. B. Cranfield, *The Epistle to the Romans*, vol. I, *The International Critical Commentary* (Edinburgh: T. & T. Clark, 1975), 431.

[13] Bruce A. Ware, *God's Lesser Glory: The Diminished God of Open Theism* (Wheaton, Ill.: Crossway Books, 2000), 102–21.

picture of a loving God choosing to save the unworthy. Arminians will pick up primarily on the theme of divine omniscience, which would, of course, include God's foreknowledge of our future decisions. A *synthesis* of these competing perspectives is needed. In addition, we must not forget that the ultimate goal of this divine foreknowledge and predestination is: (1) that we be conformed to the image of Christ; (2) that we become the church, the family of God with the mutual affection of siblings; and (3) that we experience God's glory. All true believers have been called and justified, and we will be glorified. Let us make sure, whatever our conviction,—Calvinist or Arminian—that we fully cooperate with God in his conforming us to the image of Christ and in his forming us into his church, his family, the body of Christ (Rom. 8:29–30).

Another key passage to be considered in our study of election and predestination is Ephesians 1:3–14. This majestic Trinitarian hymn is one long sentence in the Greek. It divides neatly into three stanzas, devoted respectively to the Father, the Son, and the Holy Spirit. The lines of demarcation, working directly from the Greek text, are: (1) "to the praise of the glory of his grace" (v. 6); (2) "to the praise of his glory" (v. 12); (3) "to the praise of his glory" (v. 14). This is a *grace* hymn par excellence! We are pointed to God's "glorious grace" (or lit. "the glory of his grace," v. 6), with which God has "blessed" (from the *char* root; compare *charis*, grace) us. And we are reminded of "the riches of his grace" (v. 7), which God has lavished upon us. The comprehensive vision of our redemption which Paul provides us here is founded solely on divine grace.

This is also a *Christ* hymn. He is mentioned in virtually every verse, and it is only *in him*—a phrase repeated some eleven times—that we receive all of these blessings of salvation. The Father himself is the subject of the hymn. He is the one who blesses us (v. 3), redeems us (v. 7), and seals us (v. 13). And the Holy Spirit himself is the one who brings the confident assurance of our salvation (vv. 13–14).

In terms of our doctrinal focus, we must note that it is always "in Christ" that we are chosen (elected) and predestined (vv. 4–5, 11). No theologian has more forcefully brought this point home than Karl Barth. The message of the entire Ephesian letter is that, in terms of our salvation: (1) God does it all; (2) he does it through Christ; and (3) he does it for the church. In fact, Christ and the church are mentioned in virtually every verse of the epistle.[14] Barth elaborates these themes in the more than five hundred pages he devotes to the biblical doctrine of election.[15]

First, in a pluralistic age such as ours, Barth's voice needs to be heard again: There is no salvation outside of Jesus Christ!

> That we know God and have God only in Jesus Christ means that we can know Him and have Him only with the man Jesus of Nazareth and with the people which He represents. Apart from this man and apart from this people God would be a different, an alien God. According to the Christian perception He would not be God at all.[16]

Special grace and the doctrines of election and predestination point to the supremacy of Christ: "There is salvation in no one else, for there is no other name under heaven given among mortals by which we must be saved" (Acts 4:12). Only special revelation is saving revelation. General revelation in creation and conscience merely hold us accountable. The same is true with grace. There *is* a common grace shared by all persons. But special grace alone is saving grace, and this grace is received through Christ alone.

Second, Barth would remind us that election, rightly understood, is the essence of the gospel. And it is a joyous message. It is not a mixed message of triumph and terror.[17] The Christmas angels brought "good news of great joy for all the people" (Luke 2:10). Too often the theologians have corrupted the message with their speculations on God's eternal counsels. Then election becomes a problem and the damnation of the

---

[14] See Dale Moody, *Christ and the Church: An Exposition of Ephesians with Special Application to Some Present Issues* (Grand Rapids, Mich.: Eerdmans, 1963).

[15] Karl Barth, *Church Dogmatics*, II/2 (Edinburgh: T. & T. Clark, 1957), 1–506.

[16] Barth, *Church Dogmatics*, II/2, 7.

[17] See Barth, *Church Dogmatics* II/2, 10–14.

lost eclipses the salvation of the elect. In this Ephesian passage Barth sees "not only the electing God but also the elected man."[18] He sees Christ himself as the key to election and predestination.

As I have written elsewhere: "The progression of Barth's thought on this subject is (1) the election of Jesus Christ, (2) the election of the community, and (3) the election of the individual.... Jesus Christ is the Elect One (Is. 42:1; Matt. 12:18; Luke 9:35), and the church is elect in him, as the opening hymn in Ephesians so beautifully expresses it!"[19] In this way, in my opinion, Barth has captured the essence of the New Testament doctrines of election and predestination. But Barth's concept of grace, in the end, was too optimistic. He hoped for a universal salvation of humankind, which the Scriptures simply do not promise.

Perhaps the most hotly debated of all the Pauline passages on this subject, however, would be chapters 9–11 of Romans. The overall concern of these chapters, which should be read together as a unit, is the place of Israel in God's plan of redemption. Has God failed with Israel? Has he jettisoned Israel for rejecting Christ? Has the church, as it were, supplanted Israel? Paul agonized over these questions, being a son of Israel himself. The key word for these chapters (and for the exhortation which follows: Rom. 12:1-2) is *mercy*.[20] God's sovereign saving plans are still in place, Paul informs us. Israel's exclusion of Christ simply resulted in the Gentiles *inclusion*! But the Gentiles who welcomed Christ need not feel superior. After all, they have merely been "cut from what is by nature a wild olive tree and grafted, contrary to nature, into a cultivated olive tree" (Rom. 11:24). And God still has glorious plans in place for a mighty harvest among the Jews. But Paul's opening words in this section are troubling to some.

What exactly is Paul saying in Romans 9:6-33? Is he arguing that since God is free to do as he pleases, that he has the right to chose some for salvation and ignore the rest? Some interpreters, using a simple,

---
[18] Barth, *Church Dogmatics*, II/2, 117.
[19] Hart, *Truth Aflame*, 446.
[20] In reading carefully through these chapters, the reader should note how many times this word is used. It truly sets the theme for this section.

straightforward reading of the text, would say yes. Very little exegesis as such is needed: "So then he has mercy on whomever he chooses, and he hardens the heart of whomever he chooses" (v. 18). And we have no right as his creatures to argue with God about this arrangement (compare, e.g., vv. 19–21). Unfortunately, open theists have used a similar hermeneutic to argue for God's limited knowledge of the future. Some texts, read with this same "natural" hermeneutic, can be understood as teaching just that! Most often, especially with such crucial texts, we need to do more in-depth exegetical work and compare scripture with scripture. But even then, in this particular instance, interpreters have come up with differing results. Since the church has never reached a consensus, should there be a tolerance, therefore, of honest differences? The obvious answer is yes.

The final result is an ongoing debate between two major camps. Calvinists, emphasizing the *sovereignty* of God, take Paul to be teaching unconditional election and irresistible grace in this passage. Arminians, emphasizing the *love* of God, would argue that Calvinists have "missed the forest for the trees" here. Paul's overall argument in these three chapters, they would say, is that God's mercy is available to all. Yes, God does utilize even the *unbelief* of his people (Israel) to accomplish his sovereign purposes![21] As indicated earlier, the two positions need each other. In their extremes each position can become truly problematic to the church.

Most of us have encountered examples of these extremes. A new convert to Calvinism initially becomes more passive about evangelism, since "God is going to save whomever he chooses anyway." A young Arminian saint has such a sense of human responsibility that they fall into the trap of thinking that in effect they are saving themselves (and others) by their ongoing efforts. More seasoned saints in each tradition can balance out such immaturity and distortion. But the most important insight to be gained by these scenarios is that *our given traditions*

---

[21] For a fair, manageable, and informative explanation and comparison of the two views see: Gregory A. Boyd and Paul R. Eddy, *Across the Spectrum: Understanding Issues in Evangelical Theology* (Grand Rapids, Mich.: Baker, 2002), 132–45.

each have their inherent weaknesses. Healthy church life, as we shall see in the final chapter, is much like a healthy marriage. It often takes opposites to balance each other out. The problem is that in marriage opposites often attract (introverts being drawn to extroverts, for example) whereas in church they repel (usually by means of a church split or something similar)!

Thomas C. Oden sees a growing consensus across the ecclesial traditions, similar (on the major doctrinal issues) to that of the patristic church. In some ways his conclusions seem to bypass the Calvinism/Arminianism divide in relation to the doctrines of grace. Probably Arminians would be happier with Oden's comments on Romans 9–11 which follow than Calvinists. But in my view, he is pointing us in the right direction:

> Paul was not sorrowful because God had from eternity by an inflexible decree of reprobation damned some to death. Rather, he was sorrowful because *so many of God's own called people were willfully rejecting God's own coming.* Nor was Paul anguished because God had failed to keep promises to the descendants of Abraham, because they were failing to respond freely to God's promise-keeping. Yet they remained the people of promise, recipients of covenant, of election, Torah, and temple. "It is not as though God's word had failed. For not all who are descended from Israel are Israel" (Rom. 9:6).... The subject of the discourse in Romans 9–11 was not the eternal election or reprobation of particular individual persons to eternal life or death, as individualistic exegesis has sometimes argued, but rather the election of the Gentiles to be recipients of the promise equally with the descendants of Abraham, based on faith's response to grace.[22]

A brief review of the major tenets of each camp will demonstrate where the sticking points persist.

Traditional Calvinism is known for the acronym TULIP, which can be displayed as follows:

---

[22] Oden, *The Transforming Power of Grace*, 142–43.

> **T**otal depravity of humankind in sin
> **U**nconditional election as predestination apart from foreseen merit
> **L**imited atonement in which Christ dies only for the elect
> **I**rresistible grace which guarantees the salvation of the elect
> **P**erseverance of the saints which expresses their continuing in faith to the end

The logic of this system appeals to many. It is linear, coherent, and seemingly biblical. But *is* it totally biblical? Jacob Arminius (1560–1609) was one of the first to challenge this system, which goes back to Theodore Beza (1519–1605), Calvin's successor. Calvin would probably not put nearly the weight on predestination that Beza did (as the rational principle for a theological system). Arminians would generally accept the total depravity doctrine, which acknowledges original sin. But the rest of the points would be challenged.

Arminians would affirm the biblical doctrine of election, but would view election biblically as based on foreseen faith (conditional election). Further, Christ's atoning death would be seen not only as sufficient for the salvation of all, but also as an atonement available to all (universal atonement). Grace would be resistible in the Arminian understanding. And, finally, someone might even choose to fall from grace rather than persevere in the faith.[23]

There are variations within each camp, but those are the broad parameters for each. There is a third option, however. I was raised in Bible belt West Texas in Southern Baptist churches and was taught this view throughout my growing up years. It is a grass roots theology held by perhaps the vast majority (95%?) of Southern Baptists, even though professors in Baptist schools might hold more to Calvinistic models. Perhaps because of the strong emphasis on missions and evangelism, grass roots Southern Baptist theology gradually became more "Arminianized." Most Baptists I know in the local churches—and many if not most of their pastors—are one-point Calvinists. They have held

---

[23] I provide much more detail on these matters in *Truth Aflame*, 441–51.

on to that fifth point of Calvinism, perseverance of the saints—better known in Baptist circles as the security of the believer or "once saved always saved."[24]

As I wrote down my own theology and reflected on my pilgrimage, I became filled with gratitude for my spiritual upbringing. Here is my personal conclusion:

> In my humble opinion, I was taught the best of both traditions (Calvinism and Arminianism): Christ died for everyone; salvation is offered to everyone; God gives us the choice; our salvation is assured—in general, God does the saving from start to finish, but refuses to coerce us to accept his gift of salvation in Christ![25]

I respect those who differ with me. In fact, I quote Calvin more than any other theologian in my systematic theology, along with leading Calvinistic theologians, whose work I sincerely admire. Arminians would want to challenge me, however, on that last point: perseverance of the saints. Thus, we will conclude with a brief assessment of assurance and apostasy.

Assurance and Apostasy

We are raising one of the most important grace issues now. Can a believer have complete assurance of eternal life? If so, on what basis? Can a believer ever leave their saving union with Christ and be lost eternally? If so, can there really be assurance of eternal life? In other words, we need to explore what some theologians have called *preserving grace*.

Romans, again, is a good place to start. In the culminating words of the eighth chapter we read that literally *nothing* could ever separate us from God's love (Rom. 8:38–39). Just a few pages later, however, the apostle warns of the danger of being "cut off" (Rom. 11:22). How do we correlate these warnings and assurances sprinkled throughout the Scriptures? Jesus' parables of the wedding banquet and the soils, which

---
[24] See Bill J. Leonard, *God's Last and Only Hope: The Fragmentation of the Southern Baptist Convention* (Grand Rapids, Mich.: Eerdmans, 1990), 67.
[25] Hart, *Truth Aflame*, 448.

we have already examined, are relevant to these questions. We all agonize over the defection of friends from the faith community, just as Paul's heart went out to his own people, the Jews. One thinks of the poignant story of Chuck Templeton, who was a preaching partner with Billy Graham during their Youth for Christ days. Templeton ultimately left the faith and became a self-proclaimed agnostic. Lee Strobel relates a moving interview with Templeton in Strobel's classic, *The Case for Faith*.[26] Jesus' wedding banquet story (Matt. 22:1–14) reminds us that the true chosen of God are the ones who follow through on the call of Christ. "The king had not predetermined the decisions of those who turned down the invitation or of those who accepted it. Becoming part of the 'chosen' had been their choice all along."[27] God's ultimate decision is that even though he loves us all, only people of faith will be saved.[28] And the parable of the soils (Matt. 13:1–23; Mark 4:1–20; Luke 8:4–15) teaches us that people's response to the gospel will be varied and that some simply will not persevere.

The question then becomes, What is the spiritual state of someone who apparently had a sincere faith but departs from it? Was their faith really sincere or was it defective from the start? Predictably, two camps (at least) have emerged. One camp would put the accent on the continuing nature of faith and the serious warnings of the Bible against apostasy, understood as leaving one's saving union with Christ and being eternally lost. The other camp would stress more the assurances of Scripture that God can be trusted to finish what he has begun in our lives. Thus, those who fall away from the faith would be seen as having a spurious faith from the outset. The letter to the Hebrews provides an excellent test case on this issue. It is where most of the theological discussion on these issues ends up focusing its attention.

Hebrews issues at least five blistering warnings against apostasy: Hebrews 2:1–4; 3:7–4:13; 5:11–6:20; 10:19–39; and 12:1–29. Chapter six

---

[26] Lee Strobel, *The Case for Faith: A Journalist Investigates the Toughest Objections to Christianity* (Grand Rapids, Mich.: Zondervan, 2000), 7–18.
[27] Gilbert Bilezikian, *Christianity 101* (Grand Rapids, Mich.: Zondervan, 1993), 151.
[28] Bilezikian, *Christianity 101*, 153.

warns of "those who have once been enlightened, and have tasted the heavenly gift, and shared in the Holy Spirit, and have tasted the goodness of the word of God and the powers of the age to come, and then have fallen away" (Heb. 6:4–6). These people, says the writer, are "impossible to restore to repentance" and are facing a final judgment (vv. 4, 6–8). Could there be a more dire warning! The other four warnings in this letter are just as stringent. And yet, each is also followed by a word of encouragement. In fact, the whole epistle was intended as a word of encouragement (Heb. 13:22). In this particular case, the writer quickly adds, "Even though we speak in this way, beloved, we are confident of better things in your case, things that belong to salvation" (Heb. 6:9). Then what would be the purpose of these warnings?

The simplest approach is to take the simplest reading of the text. Apostasy, as a departure from Christ, is fatal. I. Howard Marshall, a Methodist New Testament scholar, concludes that "a Christian may be saved and then lost through deliberate apostasy."[29] Another argument is that a person simply loses their rewards should they apostatize. Thomas R. Schreiner and Ardel B. Caneday have provided the most thorough analysis of all the options, including their own unique contribution.[30] These authors conclude that the warnings are real, not bluffs, and are used by God to keep the elect on the right track. Anyone who does apostatize, however, was never truly elect (a Calvinistic perspective). Either side of the issue can make a strong biblical case. We are at another impasse then when it comes to preserving grace. The extremes of these two positions cause the most problems. Extreme Calvinism tends toward determinism in which human responsibility in this area could be largely ignored. Extreme Arminianism, on the other hand, puts such an emphasis on human responsibility that a believer's destiny seems largely to be determined by their religious performance. The balance would lie somewhere between these two extremes of determinism and humanism.

---

[29] I. Howard Marshall, *Kept by the Power of God: A Study of Perseverance and Falling Away* (Minneapolis, Minn.: Bethany Fellowship, 1969), 145.

[30] Thomas R. Schreiner and Ardel B. Caneday, *The Race Set Before Us: A Biblical Theology of Perseverance & Assurance* (Downers Grove, Ill.: InterVarsity Press, 2001).

A classic Baptist position would maintain that God's preserving grace works this way: God does not save us in spite of our backslidings; rather, he draws us back to him in repentance and renewed faith, enlisting the human will in the process—like a Good Shepherd![31]

Preserving grace also entails a true assurance of faith. God's Word unequivocally states that we can *know* that we have eternal life: 1 John 5:13. Jesus Christ our Savior and Lord is the Good Shepherd who gives us complete assurances of our security: "I give them eternal life, and they will never perish. No one will snatch them out of my hand" (John 10:28). Paul knew this divinely given assurance: "I know the one in whom I have put my trust, and I am sure that he is able to guard until that day what I have entrusted to him" (2 Tim. 1:12). Paul communicated this same assurance to his Philippian readers: "I am confident of this, that the one who began a good work among you will bring it to completion by the day of Jesus Christ" (Phil. 1:6). Unlike us, God always finishes what he starts!

The apostle Peter knew that the Christian life was a confident pilgrimage into the brightest of futures, and that we "are being protected by the power of God through faith for a salvation ready to be revealed in the last time" (1 Peter 1:5). And he would also exhort us to be "eager to confirm [our] call and election" through a diligent life of spiritual growth (2 Peter 1:3–11). Paul's way of encouraging sincere discipleship through preserving grace would be to exhort us to "work out your own salvation with fear and trembling; for it is God who is at work in you, enabling you both to will and to work for his good pleasure" (Phil. 2:12–13). Jude's serious warnings against spiritual danger are

---

[31] See Hart, *Truth Aflame*, 456–57, echoing the sage advice of E. Y. Mullins.

concluded with these comforting words: "Now to him who is able to keep you from falling, and to make you stand without blemish in the presence of his glory with rejoicing, to the only God our Savior, through Jesus Christ our Lord, be glory, majesty, power, and authority, before all time and now and forever. Amen" (Jude 24–25). Finally, the Holy Spirit himself brings true assurance of faith through his internal witness to our spirits that we truly belong to God (Rom. 8:16; Gal. 4:6; 1 John 4:13; 5:10). But how does one correlate these assurances with the apostasy warnings?

First, the warnings should be taken with the utmost seriousness. Sin is not measles; it is cancer. It pays only one wage: death (Rom. 6:23). Sin tolerated in our lives darkens our minds, hardens our hearts, and alienates us from God (Eph. 4:18). It is *always* destructive. We will reap what we sow (Gal. 6:7–8). It is always spiritually perilous to live in unbelief, indifference, and disobedience.

Second, we should encourage one another in the Christian pilgrimage—the very point of the letter to the Hebrews. This naturally leads us to an examination of how God's grace is lived out in the Christian community, which will be the topic of our last chapter. Third, we should seek out those who have strayed from the church. They need a tough love that accepts them unconditionally, yet warns of spiritual peril. A test case will illumine the pastoral dynamics here.

Ten years ago Joe Smith was an active member of our church. But for the last decade he has gone back to living as he did before his conversion. What should we conclude about him, and what should we do? John Piper, a Calvinist, once warned a man who professed to be a believer that he would go to hell if he did not fight against the sin of adultery and return to his wife.[32] Of course, Piper would conclude that if that man failed to heed the warning and died in that sinful state that he was never truly elect anyway. But what substantive difference is there between the kind of advice that Piper gave and what the average Wesleyan pastor would

---

[32] John Piper, *Future Grace* (Sisters, Ore.: Multnomah, 1995), 331.

counsel? Both would agree that the man was in spiritual peril. Both would warn him severely.

Our speculation on these matters is often in vain. The Calvinist might look at someone who no longer professes faith and conclude that they never truly believed. The Arminian might conclude that the person had truly been saved but had now apostatized. *In either case*, the obvious need is to pursue that person and warn of their spiritual peril! Therefore, either view on this issue can be argued for, but the strategy for rescue is the same.

Thus, the most important issue to resolve would be how one can have an authentic assurance of faith. How can we know that if we died today that we would be in the presence of the Lord? Both a mature Calvinism and a mature Arminianism would be able to affirm and utilize the above mentioned biblical promises. But extremes of these positions could never reach full assurance of faith. The extreme Calvinist might conclude that the only real evidence that they are elect is that they persevere to the end: And they simply do not know that that will be the case, so they cannot be sure that they have eternal life. The extreme Arminian, saved one day and lost the next, surely lacks in assurance: How can they know that they will "time it right" in terms of death or the return of Christ and be in a saved state on that momentous day? Thus, Calvin and Wesley are often much closer than Calvinism and Wesleyanism (Arminianism). Wesley himself once wrote that the "truth of the Gospel is within a hairsbreadth of Calvinism."[33]

Therefore, a robust and biblical basis for an authentic understanding of God's preserving grace can be had by all. We can avoid both a cheap grace which entails no discipleship and a false piety by which a person attempts to pull themselves up by their own spiritual boot straps. One major concern remains to be addressed. How do we live out God's grace in relation to fellow believers and in relation to our unbelieving neighbor? This will be the focus of our next chapter.

---

[33] See Marshall, *Kept by the Power of God*, back cover.

Chapter Seven:
Grace and God's People

UNLESS GRACE IMPACTS PEOPLE, it is not grace. It is an attribute of God, descriptive of how he relates to fallen humanity. It is also God's saving activity on our behalf. But finally, grace characterizes the attitudes and actions of God's people. It points to the myriad ways that God manifests himself through his people. It is the dynamic behind all the ways in which God's people interact with each other and come together to form the people of God. It also *should* characterize how we relate to the world around us. The greatest obstacle to the church's mission is what Philip Yancey would call "ungrace."[1]

Ungrace describes the lovelessness that too often characterizes those who claim to belong to God. It refers as well to unforgiveness in all its forms. Failure to follow through on the Great Commandment (love) leads to failure to fulfill the Great Commission (discipling the nations). Most stagnant churches are not experiencing healthy growth because of a failure to love. They lack the power and impact which only divine grace, active in them and through them, can generate. Therefore, in this final chapter we want to explore some of the fundamental ways that grace is manifested in the attitudes and actions of God's people. In addition, we want to examine what I call the "grace-basis for Christian living."

Most Christians have at least some appreciation for the grace at work in their conversion. What they too often lack is an understanding of how it is only by that same grace that they can actually *live* the Christian life. We are justified by grace (through faith): Most believers have been taught that. But it is only by the grace of God that we can make progress in sanctification and persevere in the Christian pilgrimage:

---

[1] Yancey's treatment of grace is already a classic: *What's So Amazing About Grace?* (Grand Rapids, Mich.: Zondervan, 1997).

Many have *not* been taught that. Therefore, in this final chapter, grace gets *personal*! We will have to reexamine virtually every dimension of Christian living. The first topic for discussion will be our relation to outsiders.

Outsiders

"Conduct yourselves wisely toward outsiders," Paul exhorted the Colossians, "making the most of the time. Let your speech always be gracious [lit. with grace], seasoned with salt, so that you may know how you ought to answer everyone" (Col. 4:5–6). Conduct toward outsiders—something perhaps most Christians worry little about. And yet, if we have truly experienced grace, then surely our first impulse would be to share that grace with others. Therefore, one of the first ways that grace manifests itself in our lives is in the arena of our conversations and relationships with outsiders. The first thing that is needed is *wisdom*.

We are to "walk in wisdom toward outsiders" (v. 5, literal rendering), Paul says. Christians too often come across as patently *ungracious*. We announce to the nation, as my own denomination actually did, that we are going after the Jews with the gospel. We *should* be eager to share the gospel with the Jewish community. But is it a wise strategy to make a public announcement of our intentions? If we were Jewish, how would we feel about such an announcement? Would it open us up to the Christian message or merely make us more defensive? Paul had a completely opposite approach. He chose to be a servant of all people, becoming as a Jew to the Jews—"all things to all people"—in order that he "might by all means save some" (1 Cor. 9:19–23).

Second, wisdom entails making the most of our opportunities, "redeeming the time" (v. 5, literal rendering). People of grace are sensitized by God to the urgency of time. The end of the world might not be today, but for the millions who die today it *is* the end of the world for them. Are they ready to enter eternity? Sadly, most are not. I tell my seminary students that most of them don't really believe in hell. They predictably respond with disagreement. Then I add, "If you really believed in hell, then you would be doing everything you could, as often as you could, to avert people from going there." Again, grace experienced also means grace shared.

Our very words are crucial in this process: Paul says that they should be "always with grace, seasoned with salt, so that you may know how to answer everyone" (v. 6, literal rendering). The first key word is *always*. What a challenge! Always alert! Always on guard! Always eager to share grace! Our Lord has commissioned us for this very lifestyle (Matt. 28:18–20). Next, our words should be "with [or in] grace" (v. 6). Gracious speech is pleasant speech. It communicates by its very demeanor the grace of God. It makes the things of God attractive. It treats the hearer with respect, knowing that they too have been made in the image of God. Therefore, our words will also be "seasoned with salt" (v. 6)—interesting, engaging, strategic, and influential. Eugene Peterson's paraphrase captures well this dynamic: "The goal is to bring out the best in others in a conversation, not put them down, not cut them out" (v. 6 The Message). Finally, we need to "know how [we] ought to answer everyone" (v. 6).

Gracious speech is informed speech, seasoned with knowledge that will help others. Surely, in part, this means that each of us should know how to give a meaningful presentation of the gospel of grace. Further, especially in our pluralistic culture, we should have at least an elemental training in apologetics. As Peter wrote: "Always be prepared to give an answer to everyone who asks you to give the reason for the hope that you have. But do this with gentleness and respect" (1 Peter 4:15 TNIV). At the very least, we should know which pieces of literature might be helpful to an honest inquirer. Grace means being *prepared* to help others.

Colossians' twin epistle, the letter to the Ephesians, expresses these same themes. We are to consider carefully how we are living, "not as unwise people, but as wise, making the most of the time, because the days are evil" (Eph. 5:15–16). We are to have a firm grasp on what the will of the Lord is for our lives and to live grace-filled, Spirit-filled lives (vv. 17–21). Grace brings *purpose* to our lives. The Spirit has specific ministry in mind for each of us. (More will be said about this later.) Therefore, not only in our speech, but also in our *actions* we should be ready to demonstrate divine grace.

People in Need

Grace shows compassion. Jesus Christ, grace incarnate, was the most compassionate person who ever lived. I have a vivid memory of a particular day in my freshman year in college. I was enrolled in a Southern Baptist school in Texas and sitting in my New Testament class. The professor asked, "Why did Jesus heal the sick?" We gave the predictable Baptist answers: to show us our need to be healed spiritually from sin, to show us he truly was the Messiah, and so forth. The professor replied, "Wrong! You're all wrong! Jesus healed the sick *because they were sick!*"[2] Jesus had compassion. Living in grace entails living a life of compassionate service.

At the last judgment Jesus is going to separate the sheep from the goats (Matt. 25:31–46). We all know who the goats are. But who are the sheep? How does Jesus characterize them? Judging by the prevailing conversations of most Christians I know, Jesus would say something like this:

> Come, you who are blessed by my Father! You believed in the infallibility and inerrancy of the Bible, you rejected the paltry views of those open theists, who have diminished my glory,[3] you

---

[2] Jesus' miracles did serve as signs of his kingdom and of who he was, but we should never lose sight of his compassion.
[3] Yet treating them with *grace*: compare Millard J. Erickson, *What Does God Know and When Does He Know It?* (Grand Rapids, Mich.: Zondervan, 2003), 256–57.

have remained faithful to orthodoxy in the face of liberalism, and you have spoken prophetically against the social ills of your day. Inherit the kingdom I have prepared for you.

Everything listed in the above paragraph is a good thing, in my view. But it is not what Jesus said! His true sheep, with a living faith and an authentic experience of grace, will feed the hungry, give drink to the thirsty, welcome the stranger, clothe the naked, take care of the sick, and visit those in prison. And to do that for anyone is to do it for Christ himself (Matt. 25:31–46)! Too often we have tried to *substitute* orthodoxy (right belief) for orthopraxy (right behavior), when both are essential and inseparable in a living, healthy faith.

True faith will show itself in good works (James 2:18–26). It involves such things as caring "for orphans and widows in their distress" (James 1:27). Jesus said to "let your light shine before others, so that they may see your good works and give glory to your Father in heaven" (Matt. 5:16). Works of any kind do not bring salvation, but good works *are* the true evidence of an authentic grace-enabled faith. Here is where our lives in the world and in the church merge. Living in grace entails living a life of love toward all people and being good stewards of divinely bestowed grace.

The Church

The church is the real touchstone of authentic Christianity. If it doesn't work in the local church, it doesn't work period. But it has worked for two thousand years, even though our history is far from pristine. We have yet to "arrive" and won't in this life. The teaching of the Scriptures is clear, however. We have a stewardship toward one another in God's grace. The apostle Peter's words have a contemporary ring in our day:

> The end of all things is at hand; therefore be self-controlled and sober-minded for the sake of your prayers. Above all, keep loving one another earnestly, since love covers a multitude of sins. Show hospitality to one another without grumbling. As each has

> received a gift, use it to serve one another, as good stewards of God's varied grace: whoever speaks, as one who speaks oracles of God; whoever serves, as one who serves by the strength that God supplies—in order that in everything God may be glorified through Jesus Christ. To him belong glory and dominion forever and ever. Amen (1 Peter 4:7–11 ESV).

Love is the overarching command. "By this everyone will know that you are my disciples," Jesus taught his disciples in the upper room, "if you have love for one another" (John 13:35). Each of us "has received a gift [*charisma*]," Peter says; and we are to use it for service "as good stewards of God's varied grace [*charis*]" (v. 10). A *charisma* (gift) is a concrete manifestation of *charis* (grace). And this grace is varied or manifold like the rainbow. The two broad categories Peter lists for these gifts are speaking and serving (v. 11). And the ultimate purpose of this ministry is the glory of God (v. 11).

When divine grace enters our life, we are marked for a place of ministry in the church. As Paul wrote in Romans: "Having gifts [*charismata*] that differ according to the grace [*charis*] given to us, let us use them" (Rom. 12:6 ESV). Paul gave these instructions "by the grace given to me" (Rom. 12:3 ESV). He told the Corinthians: "But each has his own gift [*charisma*] from God, one of one kind and one of another" (1 Cor. 7:7 ESV). And to the Ephesians Paul wrote, "But grace [*charis*] was given to each of us according to the measure of Christ's gift" (Eph. 4:7 ESV), going on to describe the mutual ministry we all can enjoy in Christ's body, the church (vv. 8–16). Thus, we have all received grace, and therein lies our unity. And the grace-gifts, the spiritual gifts, we receive shape our diversity. First Corinthians 12–14 develops this same unity-within-diversity theme with a portrait of the members of Christ's body being interdependent. Given this perspective there is no place for inferiority (1 Cor. 12:14–20) or superiority (vv. 21–26).

Paul's Colossians epistle beautifully depicts the ethos of healthy, grace-filled church life:

As God's chosen ones, holy and beloved, clothe yourselves with compassion, kindness, humility, meekness, and patience. Bear with one another and, if anyone has a complaint against another, forgive each other; just as the Lord has forgiven you, so you also must forgive. Above all, clothe yourselves with love, which binds everything together in perfect harmony. And let the peace of Christ rule in your hearts, to which indeed you were called in the one body. And be thankful. Let the word of Christ dwell in you richly; teach and admonish one another in all wisdom; and with gratitude in your hearts sing psalms, hymns, and spiritual songs to God. And whatever you do in word or deed, do everything in the name of the Lord Jesus, giving thanks to God the Father through him (Col. 3:12–17).

Grace manifests itself in humble, selfless service in the church. It produces a forgiving community which lives in loving harmony even when admonishment is necessary. It will be a worshiping community filled with gratitude to God. Divine grace alone can empower us to be all that we should be toward one another.

> Grace manifests itself in humble, selfless service in the church.

In this brief survey of grace in the Bible we have dealt with a number of issues that can easily cause division in the body of Christ. The Calvinism/Arminianism divide is an obvious example. We so easily divide over the leaders we are drawn to: "I am of Calvin!" "I am of Wesley!" "I am of Piper!" "I am of Pinnock!" (compare 1 Cor. 1:12). New teachings and experiences can also be an occasion for division. There is nothing more dangerous than a recent convert to Calvinism or a new charismatic. They want to convert everyone to their new discovery. Wise pastors learn to temper the over zealous and balance out their theology. Even inadvertently, we can harm a brother or sister with our teaching.

Mature Calvinists down the generations have been aware that predestination can be wrongly taught to the harm of their hearers. I vividly remember when I first heard my mentor, Dale Moody, defend strongly from the Bible the Wesleyan view of apostasy. For a period of time my sense of assurance was shaken and fear of spiritual peril enveloped me. Moody himself had nothing to do with this, and later I regained my spiritual footing. But the dangers of spiritual damage are always present when we teach. In his early years as a pastor, D. James Kennedy, the late pastor of Coral Ridge Presbyterian Church in Fort Lauderdale, Florida, would conclude that someone was simply non-elect if they failed to respond to Kennedy's gospel presentation. He would later laugh about this. And when one heard Dr. Kennedy proclaim the gospel, speculation about these issues never entered the picture. He also worked very comfortably alongside non-Calvinistic saints in the spread of the gospel. Grace means that even when such doctrinal diversity exists, we can still maintain our unity in Christ and labor together in his vineyard.

Grace and the Christian Life

Finally, we must examine the grace-basis for Christian living. Paul wrote these words to Titus:

> For the grace of God has appeared that offers salvation to all people. It teaches us to say "No" to ungodliness and worldly passions, and to live self-controlled, upright and godly lives in this present age, while we wait for the blessed hope—the appearing of the glory of our great God and Savior, Jesus Christ, who gave himself for us to redeem us from all wickedness and to purify for himself a people that are his very own, eager to do what is good (Titus 2:11–14).

We looked at these verses earlier, but the purpose of emphasizing them again is to note the sanctifying power of grace: Grace gives us the ability to say no to sin! Grace brings purity and discipline into the life of the believer. It enables us to follow through in the discipleship process.

One often hears it said that regeneration is something God does for us and, in turn, the living of the Christian life is something we do for

God in gratitude for his gift of salvation. Anyone who has been very far down that road knows that it is a dead end! Without the continuing work of God's grace we simply cannot live the Christian life: "Apart from me you can do nothing," Jesus taught us (John 15:5). Grace alone liberates us to obey.

I used to resent the fact that in my growing up years I heard only gospel messages on Sunday morning and not enough teaching on exactly how to live the Christian life. It was a legitimate gripe. But I now have a new appreciation for my heritage. When we continually hear the gospel—and share the gospel!—we are constantly reminded of the grace-basis of both our Christian life and our relationship with God. Many of us are on a performance treadmill, trying to earn God's favor, when we already have it. We have already been justified by grace through faith and have acceptance, approval, and favor with God. He will never love us more than he loves us right now. In fact, he even *likes* us, says the biblical doctrine of grace!

We can always tell when a fellow believer is treating us with Christian "politeness" and when they really love us. Some people give off the vibe that once we change to be acceptable to them—our appearance, our theology, our style of spirituality—then they will love us. Generally, these people bring out the worst in us. It is those seasoned saints who genuinely like us—love us warts and all—who liberate us to be our very best. They motivate us to further change in the right direction. God is this way in perfection.

Ultimate the reality of grace has to drop from our head to our heart. Once we are gripped by this grace in our gut, as the younger generation would say, a transformation begins to take place. Being genuinely loved is the most exhilarating experience there is. Romantic love provides a parable of this truth. The reality that someone could really love us, actually cherish us, just the way we are, amazes us. We can hardly believe it. A joy comes into our lives. A bounce comes to our step. Everyone one around us knows something wonderful has happened to us. Yes, we are loved! So it is with Christ and us. We are loved: Those three words are the essence of grace.

We are immersed in an ocean of divine love. That is the message of grace. Common grace surrounds us all. Special grace transforms the believer and prompts them to worship the God of all grace and to share the good news of God's grace with everyone. Ultimately, we are brought back, time and again, to the simplicity of the Bible's best known verse: "For God so loved the world that he gave his only Son, so that everyone who believes in him may not perish but may have eternal life" (John 3:16).

Chapter Eight: Grace and Southern Baptists

IF EVER THERE WAS A TIME for Southern Baptists to reconsider the biblical doctrine of grace it is now! The two most incendiary issues among us, Calvinism and the charismatic movement, are both "grace" issues. The biblical doctrine of grace is being debated among us as never before. Calvinists remind us of our doctrinal roots in Reformed theology and of the sovereign grace of God as the sole source of our redemption. Charismatics remind us that the grace gifts (*charismata*) are essential to fulfilling the Great Commission. The history of Baptist folk concerning these issues is not always encouraging. Perhaps this time we can actually learn from history and not repeat the same mistakes! Perhaps this time—by the grace of God—we can transcend our differences and move ahead in a renewed world mission thrust!

In one sense, it could be that our Lord is using these precise issues to gain our attention and show us our need. It would be helpful, therefore, to explore afresh a few of the key questions confronting us at present in relation to grace. First, we will examine the Calvinism issue and then the charismatic issue.

Calvinism

The reason Calvinism is an "issue" among us today is that Baptists in America, along with perhaps the vast majority of grass roots evangelicalism, have been largely "Arminianized" theologically through the wide influence of revivalism.[1] Probably the vast majority of Baptists could be

---
[1] Bill J. Leonard, *God's Last & Only Hope: The Fragmentation of the Southern Baptist Convention* (Grand Rapids: Eerdmans, 1990), 67.

characterized as "one-point Calvinists," holding faithfully to perseverance of the saints, but moving away from total depravity, unconditional election, limited atonement, and irresistible grace. This position could be fairly labeled as one form of Arminian theology. Calvinists would remind us that this development is a rather recent innovation in the total history of Baptist thought. If grass root folk view our mission as "bringing in the kingdom" on our own, Reformed saints would aver that this enterprise is the Lord's prerogative: Apart from him we can do nothing. We often evangelize in a somewhat deistic fashion, as if God has done all he's going to do and it is up to us to "get saved" and "get *them* saved." Jesus taught the opposite, however: "No one can come to me unless the Father has enabled them" (John 6:65). Grace always precedes and enables saving faith.

My mentor at Southern Baptist Theological Seminary during my M.Div. and Ph.D. days was Dale Moody. Moody became convinced that the Bible teaches a classical Arminian theology which includes the belief that one can leave their saving relationship with the Lord and be lost eternally. Needless to say, he became a lightning rod of controversy and eventually lost his teaching post at the seminary. I have poignant personal memories of those days. I had never seriously considered Moody's view of apostasy, and the thought of such a danger terrified me. My sense of assurance of faith was shaken somewhat and serious biblical and theological reflection ensued.

A Calvinist would quickly observe that such a loss of assurance is the fruit of Arminian theology. And there is much in the history of the American church to document such a concern. Unfortunately, the same issue could be raised concerning the resurgence of Calvinism. How does one really know they are elect? Must they simply wait until the end of their days—or even until the judgment itself—to determine if they have persevered and are elect? At this point a robust theology of the Holy Spirit can come to our rescue. Both Wesley and Calvin taught a strong doctrine of assurance. Grace-enabled faith is itself a decisive witness to our being elect. The Spirit bears witness with our spirit that we are God's children (Rom. 8:16). God personalizes his promises to us. The Word and Spirit work in tandem, assuring us of our filial relation with the Father. But the question of authentic assurance is only one of many that surface in the theological debates surrounding the Calvinism/Arminianism divide.

The first question we should consider is the most basic of all: Why the resurgence of Calvinism? The past few decades have witnessed a descent into ethical and theological chaos in American society as well as the church. Younger generations especially are looking for moorings. I have had the opportunity over the years to observe first hand both the Southern Baptist Convention and the charismatic movement in America. Many times I have noted how college or seminary students will gravitate toward a tradition which offers a solid interpretative grid and a sense of historical continuity. Even though postmodern tolerance offers some relief from intellectual and emotional dissonance, many still seem to gravitate toward an authoritative interpretive voice. Both Roman Catholicism and Eastern Orthodoxy have found surprisingly great appeal among these searching students. Those leaning toward staying within the evangelical fold have rediscovered their rich Reformed roots, and dynamic leaders and scholars such as John Piper, Wayne Grudem, C. J. Mahaney, Mark Dever, and Al Mohler have captured their attention and affections with a clarion call for sound doctrine and passionate discipleship in morally and spiritually compromised times.

> *The past few decades have witnessed a descent into ethical and theological chaos in American society as well as the church. Younger generations especially are looking for moorings.*

For many, rediscovering the sovereignty of God and his gracious initiative in our redemption is almost like a second conversion. He really does have everything under control! It is *God* who is saving us, and he finishes what he starts! Many become bold and aggressive witnesses to their newfound Reformed faith.

I have often said (as mentioned earlier) that there is nothing more dangerous than a new Calvinist or a new charismatic. They want to share their new discoveries with everyone they meet. They want to *convert* everyone they meet to their point of view. They can easily—though most often inadvertently—become a divisive force in the church. So can their opponents! Only mature and secure saints can weather their spiritual and theological differences: Too often we have not evidenced such sagacity.

Calvinism is not going away, and neither is the charismatic movement. So what are the key questions they raise and how should these challenges be handled? Perhaps the most important concern Calvinism raises in our day is how current culture has influenced the church toward *humanism*.

American Christianity is rife with humanism. Ironically, even our revivalism roots have nudged us in this direction with the often sole focus on the individual. Americans are pragmatists: What's in it for me? I cannot count the times I have warned my charismatic students of this weakness in the movement. A strong dose of Calvinism can help us refocus on *God*: We exist for *his* glory, not he for ours! Religious experience divorced from the mind too often evaporates, and today, thankfully, in some quarters there is a return to loving God with all our minds and being renewed in our minds (Mark 12:29–31; Rom. 12:1–2). Doctrine matters because it summarizes the teachings of the Bible which we are called upon to obey if we truly love our Lord (John 14:15). Thus, Calvinism's emphasis on "religious affections" (Edwards) conjoined with sound doctrine is a needed corrective in our day. At the same time, Calvinism raises important theological questions which demand to be addressed: What is the nature of God's sovereignty? How exactly are we saved? Is the gift of salvation available to every person?

Donald Bloesch has observed that what we often encounter today with respect to our views of God is a rampant immanentalism. There is a diminishing if not total denial of divine transcendence.[2] God's grandeur is diminished both in terms of his identity and his attributes. Is God truly sovereign over his creation and how precisely does he relate to his creation?

> *Indeterminism* says that God is not in control and, therefore, his will is not done. *Determinism* says that God's control is so absolute that in effect human freedom and responsibility are canceled. *Omnicausality* says that God does everything and his creation does nothing. *Chance* says that no personal or rational power is in control. And *fate* says that the ultimate power is not necessarily benevolent.[3]

Examples of each of these aberrations abound. All five should be avoided like the plague! Unfortunately, in the Calvinism/Arminianism debate Calvinists are often depicted as arguing for determinism or omnicausality and Arminians for indeterminism. There is some truth in both accusations.

Some forms of Arminianism are clearly Pelagian or at least semi-Pelagian. Losing and gaining one's salvation every other day—based on the success of one's practice of the faith—is clearly Pelagian. There is no gospel in this conception of the Christian life and no assurance of faith. By and large, Baptists have avoided this devious path. However, they have not always been as successful avoiding a "High Calvinism" which nudged some in the direction of a passive resignation that God will save whomever he wills and does not need the help of our own missions and evangelism efforts. True, he doesn't need our help. *But he has sovereignly chosen to use our efforts in part to bring the elect into the*

---

[2] Cf. Donald G. Bloesch, *God the Almighty Power, Wisdom, Holiness, Love* (Downers Grove, Ill.: InterVarsity Press, 1995), 17.
[3] Larry D. Hart, *Truth Aflame* (Grand Rapids, Mich.: Zondervan, 2005), 183 (adapted from Thomas C. Oden, *The Living God* [San Francisco: Harper & Row, 1987], 277–78).

kingdom! Are there indications of a resurgence of High Calvinism among Southern Baptists today? Not among the most articulate spokespersons for Reformed theology, but among grassroots folk the danger clearly lurks. Learning the lesssons of our history becomes crucial at this point.

Our earliest ancestors were already divided over the Calvinism/Arminianism question when they arrived on our shores. General Baptists were decidedly Arminian in their theological orientation, believing that Christ died for everyone (general atonement) and that anyone could choose to cooperate with divine grace and be saved. Unfortunately, these pioneers also accepted the idea of "falling away" from Christ and being lost forever, after having been saved. They were known as General Baptists because of their belief in general atonement.

In contrast, Particular Baptists followed wholeheartedly the teachings of John Calvin, believing that Christ died only for the elect, who had been chosen by God before the foundation of the world. This belief in particular atonement earned them the moniker Particular Baptists. Their Reformed faith would be widely influential in subsequent centuries as Baptists hammered out their confessional statements. Thus, our British forebears had already set the table for future theological "conversations"![4]

One important observation could be made concerning the prevailing theological orientation of grass roots Southern Baptists today. They hold to a hybrid of these two diverse theological perspectives. With the Arminians they hold to general atonement and the universal offer of salvation; and with the Calvinists they revere belief in the security of the believer. Some theologians view this as an impossible combination of beliefs. The vast majority of Southern Baptists embrace this perspective, which seems to have served them quite well. Many view this theological construct as quite biblical and empowering of Christian mission. I count myself among them.

But now the theological waters have been stirred. Leave it to ornery theology professors and pastors, like myself, to muddy the waters and

---

[4] See Bill J. Leonard, *Baptists in America* (New York: Columbia University Press, 2005), 8–10, 21–23.

complicate things with biblical, historical, and theological perspectives to "afflict the comfortable." A growing number of new pastors are now graduating from our historic seminaries steeped in Calvinism and speaking a distinctly new dialect from our pulpits. They can also cite some of today's most popular Christian leaders and writers in corroboration of their new fangled preaching. It's not really new at all. It goes back to our roots. There is legitimate alarm to be reckoned with, however. High Calvinism always looms like a specter when a legitimate resurgence of the Reformed faith emerges. Unfortunately, some in our midst in previous centuries fell victim to this aberration and turned their backs on the missionary enterprise.

Baptists have always been a missionary people, captivated by Christ's Great Commission. They have been blessed by God as a result. Some present leaders are alarmed at the resurgence of Calvinism because they know our history well. They are aware that early on, so-called Primitive Baptists opposed all missions and evangelism efforts on the basis of their High Calvinism. Is there a danger that this mistaken opinion could establish a footing among us again? Always! On the other hand, history also teaches us that this danger is by no means an inevitable outcome. Many of the finest witnessing saints— past and present, Calvinists to the core—have turned the world upside down with the gospel. Can anyone doubt the missionary passion of a John Piper, for example?

It will take grace for contemporary Southern Baptists to navigate these shoals. There is even evidence that our boat is already stuck, along with the rest of American Christianity—including the charismatic movement, to which we will turn shortly—in a shallow, comfortable, worldly "faith"

> *Baptists have always been a missionary people, captivated by Christ's Great Commission. They have been blessed by God as a result.*

which is having very little spiritual or social impact. Only divine grace can bring us together again and empower our witness and service. *We must pray for it as never before!* Surely on that we can all agree!

There are signs of hope, however. Constructive dialogue is already taking place and sound theological and pastoral proposals are already emerging from denominational leaders.[5] I tell my students that I generally learn more from people who disagree with me than from those who agree: Those who agree often simply reinforce my blind spots, while those who disagree often provide a much-needed balance and correction. God's Word clearly teaches that we *need* each other (1 Cor. 12–14; Rom. 12). Now, more than ever, we need to embrace and live out this biblical truth.

Something perhaps even more troubling than the resurgence of Calvinism, however, has been disturbing Southern Baptists for about the last four decades. I am referring to the charismatic movement, which has continued to grow in influence across the American religious scene, alongside the explosion of Pentecostalism worldwide. These are the tongues speakers in our midst. And they are like roaches—we just can't seem to get rid of them. In addition, we are discovering not only a vast subterranean charismatic force in our midst, but also a general greater friendliness toward charismatic beliefs and practices among our pastors. How does the biblical doctrine of grace inform us as to how we should handle these developments?

The Charismatic Movement

The reason I am arguing that the charismatic controversies among us are a grace issue is because of the biblical nomenclature itself. Spiritual gifts, including speaking in tongues, are referred to in the New Testament in part as *charismata*—literally grace-gifts!

---

[5] See, e.g., E. Ray Clendenen and Brad J. Waggoner (eds.), *Calvinism: A Southern Baptist Dialogue* (Nashville: Broadman & Holman, 2008); David S. Dockery, *Southern Baptist Consensus and Renewal: A Biblical, Historical, and Theological Proposal* (Nashville: Broadman & Holman, 2008); and the earlier work: Timothy George, *Amazing Grace: God's Initiative—Our Response* (Nashville: LifeWay Press, 2000).

As I have already argued, to reject spiritual gifts is ultimately to reject grace, since these phenomena are concrete manifestations of God's grace. But generally we don't reject spiritual gifts in total—just certain ones, such as healings and tongues. We've seen enough insanity in this arena both on television and in our local communities to be wary of accepting such extreme practices.

For some, the private opinion is held that "it may even be Bible, but it's just not Baptist!" They would be wrong. Early Baptist revivals evidenced such charismatic phenomena, and today some of our finest church members, pastors, missionaries, and denominational leaders speak in tongues and have witnessed present-day healings and miracles. The leading edge of modern Christianity is Pentecostal to the core, and Southern Baptists need to discover afresh how we are related to the larger Christian family, including these "signs and wonders" folk. Will we follow the sage advice of the apostle Paul to the Corinthians, who were divided over precisely the same issues (1 Cor. 12-14), or will we chart our own willful course?—a sure formula for failure.

To be sure, there are extremes we should avoid like the plague. It is those among us who are *militantly for or against speaking in tongues* who divide us. They need Pauline guidance if we are to present a united front in our end time mission. There are others preaching a "health and wealth" message which can only further debilitate our churches. In its extreme forms, it is really a demonic teaching, enmeshed in American materialism and blind to the Great Commission vision, in which we are called to *suffer* for the gospel. At the same time, charismatics can teach us how to trust God and step out in faith in ministry enterprises. God does continue to work financial miracles to enable our mission. Further, we *can* trust him to meet all our needs (not "greeds") when we follow biblical stewardship!

The biblical doctrine of grace, as we have already seen, teaches us to *act graciously* toward one another, even when we have serious differences of opinion in these matters—*especially* when we disagree about such things. This strong biblical teaching, pervasive in the New Testament, applies equally to both the Calvinism and charismatic issues of our day. Now we will really decide whether we will be people of the Book! Only if we *do* what it says will we see the results that it promises. We know the relevant chapters in the Bible—Romans 12, 1 Corinthians 12-14, Ephesians 4, 1 Peter 4, and the like. The question is: Will we do them? Will we practice unity within diversity, love and humility? Will we stay on message and on mission or step aside to batter one another with superior attitudes and divisive judgmentalism? Paul made it clear to the Corinthians that no member of Christ's Body should ever say to another, "I have no need of you." But we do it all the time. *Refusing to repent of this egregious sin can only result in missional failure.* It may be the most serious issue of our day.

The Future

Despite all these formidable challenges—and many more—the future is bright for God's people. How can anyone make such an assertion? Because the biblical doctrine of grace teaches us that God's grace is a conquering grace. He finishes what he starts. Our Lord will have a spotless Bride awaiting him when he comes. We can count on his help when we ask for it. The questions pressing upon us at present are: Will we accept the help and guidance he has already given us in his Word? Will we keep in step with the Spirit? Will we follow our Lord in authentic discipleship? Will we be eager to maintain the unity of the Spirit in the bond of peace (Eph. 4:3)? Will we tap into the limitless resources of divine grace?

Prayer for this transforming grace is the greatest need of this hour...

Postface

YOU HAVE JUST COMPLETED A STUDY of perhaps the most important subject any person could ever consider. Was the forewarning of the scandalous nature of the book well-taken? Ultimately, we are brought to the cross of Jesus Christ, which will always be a scandal to fallen humanity. But to those of us who cling to that cross it is most precious, for the world's only Savior died there for each and for all.

The following questions are provided for personal reflection on what you have read:

- Why is grace scandalous?
- What is grace?
- Why do even Christians differ on many aspects of the doctrine of grace?
- What has common grace now come to mean to you personally?
- What has special grace now come to mean to you personally?
- What specific ways have come to mind personally in terms of living out grace?
- Has your life been changed as a result of this study of grace?

Grace be with you!

Also by Larry Hart

Christianity in 3D

AN INVITATION TO VITAL CHRISTIANITY through an exploration of the practical implications of the doctrine of the Trinity, the work of the Holy Spirit, and the preaching, teaching, and healing ministry of Christ through His Body, the church.

Praise for *Christianity in 3D*

The Word, the Spirit, and the Community of Faith guide Hart's heart in this endeavor. The reader will discover a God of infinite dimensions who desires to redeem, transform, and empower us and to involve us in the work of his kingdom—preaching, teaching, and healing. Hart as an author is a scholar and an evangelist. His commitment to truth and his passion for souls merge in this volume. Indeed truth is aflame here! **—Dr. Thomson Mathew, Dean, College of Theology and Ministry, Oral Roberts University**

The life of faith is not supposed to be a dental appointment interrupted every now and again by falling asleep. Dr. Larry Hart calls us to put on the right glasses, turn them on and watch the adventure leap off the screen. Hart is a bold heart! And he summons us into the fray. A terrific book—if you're not afraid of 3D! **—Dr. Mark Rutland, Founder and President of Global Servants, Founder and Director of the National Institute of Christian Leadership**

Larry Hart of Oral Roberts University is one the most cheerful and positive Christians I have ever known. His new book, *Christianity in 3D*, glows with his personality and his joyful love of theology. A very good writer, Hart connects with the reader with a most readable summary of just who God is. If you love the Lord, you will love this book. **—Dr. Vinson Synan, Dean Emeritus, Regent University School of Divinity**

Visit **truthaflamepress.com** for more information.

www.ingramcontent.com/pod-product-compliance
Lightning Source LLC
Chambersburg PA
CBHW050554300426
44112CB00013B/1920